AF706063

CONTENTS

PAGE

From the Desk of the Editor-in-Chief v

2023-2024 ANNUAL COPYRIGHT REVIEW BY COWAN, LIEBOWITZ, & LATMAN..219

FROM THE DESK OF THE EDITOR-IN-CHIEF

We are pleased to present the annotated summary of cases from June 2023-June 2024, produced by Thomas Kjellberg and his team at Cowan, Liebowitz & Latman. The tradition of summaries of cases has been part of the journal's history from the first issue and has continued in one form or another for over seventy years. As the cases, law reviews, and other copyright-related resources grew, the question of what to do with the summaries became a serioua question, as printing costs also rose. The decision to put the second volume of the journal as a digital resource was made, and for the last few years, that is how it has proceeded. We honor this new trend for 2024. But the solution has a couple of problems. It does not preserve in the same way for the historical record these valuable resources, as they are not printed and bound with the rest of the issues. It is also challenging to have summaries for one year across two volumes. We are working to solve these problems for Volume 72. For now, enjoy the selected annotated summaries from Thomas Kjellberg. He and his team do a great service in keeping us informed.

This annotation covers from June 2023 through June 2024. The summaries are arranged by topic. All of the editorial, formatting, and production for the summaries is handled by Cowan, Liebowitz & Latman. The Copyright Society Law School Fellows team did not review for accuracy.

Elizabeth Townsend Gard
Editor-in-Chief
Journal of the Copyright Society
John E. Koerner Endowed Professor of Law
Tulane University Law School
eic@copyrightsociety.org

JOURNAL OF THE COPYRIGHT SOCIETY
(formerly BULLETIN OF THE COPYRIGHT SOCIETY OF THE U.S.A. and JOURNAL OF THE COPYRIGHT SOCIETY OF THE U.S.A.)

Published by the Copyright Society, 1 E 53rd Street, Floor 8, New York, NY 10022
Telephone: (212) 354-6401 | Website: www.copyrightsociety.org
For membership information, please visit copyrightsociety.org/membership-benefits.
Manuscripts may be submitted to eic@copyrightsociety.org

THE JOURNAL OF THE COPYRIGHT SOCIETY is published three times a year. The Society is located at 1 East 53rd Street, Floor 8, New York, NY 10022.

Copyright Society Membership
As a member of the Copyright Society, you are entitled to exclusive benefits, including reduced registration fees for networking events and Continuing Legal Education (CLE) programs, a subscription to the Journal, and many more privileges. For detailed membership information, please visit copyrightsociety.org/membership-benefits.

Journal Subscription
A subscription to the *Journal of the Copyright Society* runs from January through December and includes three issues. Subscriptions are accepted throughout the year for this period. Subscription orders received mid-year will be sent back issues, beginning with the first issue of the current volume. For detailed subscription information, please visit copyrightsociety.org/the-journal.

Note: There was a delay in publishing 71(2), and the issue was not published until Winter 2025. The articles are up to date as of the end of July 2024 and reflect the developments over the delayed period.

CITE: 71 J. COPYRIGHT SOC'Y, page no., . . . (2024).

"RECENT DEVELOPMENTS IN COPYRIGHT SELECTED ANNOTATED CASES"

by THOMAS KJELLBERG, JOELLE MILOV,
DASHA CHESTUKHIN AND JEREMY BERMAN

and

ALLISON FURNARI
PAIGE GEIER
JUSTIN KARASICK
SARAH SUE LANDAU
JOHN MIRANDA
RAPHAEL NEMES
REEMA PANGARKAR
EMILY STEIN
LYNDSEY WADDINGTON

Cowan, Liebowitz & Latman, P.C.,
114 West 47th Street, New York, NY 10036-1525,
(212) 790-9200 · www.cll.com · fax (212) 575-0671.

These annotations cover cases reported from June 2023 to June 2024.

TABLE OF CONTENTS

I. JURISDICTION AND PROCEDURAL ISSUES 236

A. Subject Matter Jurisdiction 236
B. Personal Jurisdiction and Venue 236
C. Pleadings 241
D. Standing 250
E. Miscellaneous 252

II. COPYRIGHTABILITY 253

A. Originality 253
B. Compilations and Derivative Works 258
C. Pictorial, Graphic and Sculptural Works 259
D. Miscellaneous 260

III. OWNERSHIP 261

A. Works Made for Hire 261
B. Transfer of Ownership 262
C. Termination of Transfers 262
D. Joint Works and Co-Ownership 264
E. Contracts and Licenses 267
F. Miscellaneous 273

IV. FORMALITIES 274

A. Registration 274

V. INFRINGEMENT 281

A. Access 281
B. Copying and Substantial Similarity 283
C. Contributory/Vicarious Infringement 294
D. Miscellaneous 302

VI. DEFENSES/EXEMPTIONS 305

A. Fair Use 305
B. Statute of Limitations 315
C. Res Judicata/Collateral Estoppel 321
D. Miscellaneous 321

VII. REMEDIES 322
A. Damages and Profits 322
B. Attorneys' Fees 325
C. Injunction/Impoundment 337
VIII. PREEMPTION 341
IX. DIGITAL MILLENNIUM COPYRIGHT ACT 346
X. VISUAL ARTISTS RIGHTS ACT 352

Table of Cases

Affordable Aerial Photography, Inc. v. Prop. Matters United States, LLC, No. 22-14296, 2023 U.S. Dist. LEXIS 115171 (S.D. Fla. July 5, 2023) 335

AFG Media Ltd. v. Poptrend-Official, No. 23-1840, 2023 U.S. Dist. LEXIS 230686 (W.D. Pa. Dec. 29, 2023) 259, 339

Alkam Home Fashion, Inc. v. Decor, No. 23-1177, 2023 U.S. Dist. LEXIS 169612 (C.D. Cal. Sept. 22, 2023) 278

Am. Airlines, Inc. v. Spada, No. 23-21844, 2024 U.S. Dist. LEXIS 32525 (S.D. Fla. Feb. 23, 2024) 247

Am. Soc'y for Testing & Materials v. Pub. Resource.Org, Inc., 82 F.4th 1262 (D.C. Cir. 2023) 305

Ambrosetti v. Or. Cath. Press, No. 21-211, 2024 U.S. Dist. LEXIS 45085 (D. Or. Mar. 13, 2024) 292

Antony v. Buena Vista Books, Inc., No. 18-205, 2024 U.S. Dist. LEXIS 9918 (E.D. Ky. Jan. 19, 2024) 282, 294

Atticus Ltd. Liab. Co. v. Dramatic Publ'g Co., No. 22-10147, 2023 U.S. Dist. LEXIS 195527 (S.D.N.Y. Oct. 31, 2023) 329

August Image, LLC v. Girard Ent. & Media LLC, No. 23-1492, 2024 U.S. Dist. LEXIS 59790 (S.D.N.Y. Apr. 1, 2024) 308

August Image, LLC v. Trend Hunter Inc., No. 22-7120, 2023 U.S. Dist. LEXIS 162807 (C.D. Cal. Sept. 12, 2023) 244

Barnes v. Jack Porter, Inc., No. 22-4633, 2023 U.S. Dist. LEXIS 171542 (D.S.C. Sep. 26, 2023) 252

Baronius Press Ltd.. v. Faithlife Corp., No. 22-1635, 2024 U.S. Dist. LEXIS 17194 (W.D. Wash. Jan. 31, 2024) 259

Beard v. Helman,
No. 21-680, 2024 U.S. Dist. LEXIS 39622
(M.D. Pa. Mar. 6, 2024)....266

Best Carpet Values, Inc. v. Google, LLC,
90 F.4th 962
(9th Cir. 2024)....341

BMG Rts. Mgmt. (United States) LLC v. Joyy Inc.,
No. 22-1578, 2024 U.S. Dist. LEXIS 25438
(C.D. Cal. Feb. 12, 2024)....243

Bold Ltd. v. Rocket Resume, Inc.,
No. 22-1045, 2023 U.S. Dist. LEXIS 108212
(N.D. Cal. June 22, 2023)....344

Bridgeport Music, Inc. v. TufAmerica, Inc.,
No. 19-1764, 2023 U.S. Dist. LEXIS 159845
(S.D.N.Y. Sep. 10, 2023)....316

Campbell v. Gannett Co.,
No. 21-557, 2023 U.S. Dist. LEXIS 142188
(W.D. Mo. Aug. 15, 2023)....313, 350

Chaquico v. Jefferson Starship, Inc.,
No. 22-4907, 2024 U.S. Dist. LEXIS 53153
(N.D. Cal. Mar. 25, 2024)....270

Chosen Figure LLC v. Kevin Frazier Prods.,
No. 22-06518, 2023 U.S. Dist. LEXIS 125669
(C.D. Cal. July 19, 2023)....310

Concord Music Grp., Inc. v. X Corp.,
No. 23-606, 2024 U.S. Dist. LEXIS 38239
(M.D. Tenn. Mar. 5, 2024)....300

Cooley v. Marcus,
No. 23-86, 2023 U.S. Dist. LEXIS 127119
(W.D. Mich. July 24, 2023)....311, 322

Covetrus Inc. v. Actian Corp.,
No. 21-97, 2023 U.S. Dist. LEXIS 176646
(D. Me. Oct. 2, 2023)....281

cPanel, LLC v. Asli,
No. 22-1963, 2024 U.S. Dist. LEXIS 1746
(D. Ore. Jan. 3, 2024)....340

Crabtree v. Kirkman,
No. 22-180, 2023 U.S. Dist. LEXIS 209380
(C.D. Cal. Nov. 22, 2023)....318, 321

Cramer v. Netflix, Inc.,
No. 22-131, 2023 U.S. Dist. LEXIS 165510
(W.D. Pa. Sept. 18, 2023)....311

Critical Response Grp., Inc. v. Geo-Comm, Inc.,
No. 22-342, 2023 U.S. Dist. LEXIS 218414
(S.D. Iowa Nov. 20, 2023) 293

Davis v. ABC,
No. 22-5944, 2024 U.S. Dist. LEXIS 48187
(S.D.N.Y. Mar. 19, 2024) 236, 285

Dermansky v. Hayride Media, LLC,
No. 22-3491, 2023 U.S. Dist. LEXIS 168076
(E.D. La. Sept. 21, 2023) 314, 351

Dermansky v. Young Turks, Inc.,
No. 22-345, 2023 U.S. Dist. LEXIS 114797
(D. Del. July 5, 2023)..240

Dermansky v. Young Turks, Inc.,
No. 23-5868, 2023 U.S. Dist. LEXIS 199258
(C.D. Cal. Nov. 3, 2023)..318

Design Gaps, Inc. v. Hall,
No. 23-186, 2023 U.S. Dist. LEXIS 208773
(W.D.N.C. Nov. 21, 2023)..345

Desirous Parties Unlimited Inc. v. Right Conn. Inc.,
No. 21-1838, 2024 U.S. Dist. LEXIS 40058
(D. Nev. Mar. 6, 2024)..258

DISH Network L.L.C. v. Jadoo TV, Inc.,
No. 20-1891, 2023 U.S. Dist. LEXIS 102984
(N.D. Cal. June 13, 2023) 298, 303

Dmarcian, Inc. v. DMARC Advisor BV,
No. 21-67, 2023 U.S. Dist. LEXIS 102010
(W.D.N.C. June 12, 2023) 279

Doorage, Inc. v. Blue Crates, LLC,
No. 20-421, 2023 U.S. Dist. LEXIS 170297
(N.D. Ill. Sep. 22, 2023)..290

Eggleston v. Twentieth Century Fox Film Corp.,
No. 21-11171, 2023 U.S. Dist. LEXIS 176139
(E.D. Mich. Sept. 29, 2023)..345

Elgin Separation Sols., LLC v. Dillon,
No. 23-440, 2023 U.S. Dist. LEXIS 184499
(S.D. W. Va. Oct. 13, 2023)..341

Elohim Epf United States, Inc. v. 162 D & y Corp.,
No. 19-2431, 2023 U.S. Dist. LEXIS 224891
(S.D.N.Y. Dec. 18, 2023)..268, 277

Elohim Epf United States, Inc. v. 600 N. Vt. Inc.,
No. 22-7516, 2023 U.S. Dist. LEXIS 127665
(C.D. Cal. June 15, 2023) 289

Enos v. Walt Disney Co.,
No. 23-5790, 2024 U.S. Dist. LEXIS 39705
(C.D. Cal. Mar. 4, 2024) 260, 288

Enter. Mgmt. Ltd., Inc. v. Construx Software Builders, Inc.,
73 F.4th 1048
(9th Cir. 2023)...274

Estate of Worrell v. Thang, Inc.,
No. 22-11009, 2024 U.S. Dist. LEXIS 11833
(E.D. Mich. Jan. 23, 2024)...251

Facility Guidelines Inst., Inc. v. Upcodes, Inc.,
677 F. Supp. 3d 955
(E.D. Mo. 2023)...313

Fashion Nova, LLC v. Blush Mark, Inc.,
No. 22-6127, 2023 U.S. Dist. LEXIS 114601
(C.D. Cal. June 30, 2023) 349

Fernandez v. Jagger,
No. 23-891, 2023 U.S. Dist. LEXIS 186839
(E.D. La. Oct. 17, 2023)...240

Fomo Factory, LLC v. Gallery Model Homes, Inc.,
No. 21-1022, 2023 U.S. Dist. LEXIS 130703
(S.D. Tex. July 28, 2023)...257, 291

Gaede v. Delay,
Nos. 23-35217, 23-35531, 2024 U.S. App. LEXIS 5389
(9th Cir. Mar. 6, 2024) 326

Gordon v. Kaiser Found. Health Plan, Inc.,
No. 23-1507, 2023 U.S. Dist. LEXIS 223921
(S.D. Cal. Dec. 15, 2023)...342

Halperin v. Goodman,
No. 20-7616, 2024 U.S. Dist. LEXIS 16026
(N.D. Ill. Jan. 30, 2024) 266

Hanagami v. Epic Games, Inc.,
85 F.4th 931
(9th Cir. 2023)...253

HCL Techs. Ltd. v. Atos S.E.,
No. 23-868, 2024 U.S. Dist. LEXIS 44038
(N.D. Tex. Mar. 12, 2024) 344

Hines v. BMG Rights Mgmt. (US) LLC,
No. 20-3535, 2023 U.S. Dist. LEXIS 170372
(S.D.N.Y. Sept. 25, 2023)...255, 287

Hunley v. Instagram, LLC,
73 F.4th 1060
(9th Cir. 2023)....294

Id Tech. LLC v. Toggle Web Media LLC,
No. 20-5949, 2023 U.S. Dist. LEXIS 182266
(E.D.N.Y. Oct. 10, 2023)....331

In Lux Rsch. v. Hull McGuire PC,
No. 23-523, 2023 U.S. Dist. LEXIS 166700
(D.D.C. Sept. 19, 2023)....246, 299

In Lux Rsch. v. Hull McGuire PC,
No. 23-523, 2024 U.S. Dist. LEXIS 31848
(D.D.C. Feb. 26, 2024)....310

In re Frontier Communs. Corp.,
No. 20-22476, slip op.
(S.D.N.Y. Bankr. Mar. 27, 2024)....297

InfoGroup Inc. v. Office Depot, Inc.,
No. 23-80358, 2023 U.S. Dist. LEXIS 106276
(S.D. Fla. June 20, 2023)....251, 304

Infogroup Inc. v. Office Depot, Inc.,
No. 23-80358, 2023 U.S. Dist. LEXIS 197980
(S.D. Fla. Nov. 3, 2023)....333

Infogroup Inc. v. Office Depot, Inc.,
No. 23-80358, 2024 U.S. Dist. LEXIS 50246
(S.D. Fla. Mar. 12, 2024)....333

JBrick, LLC v. Chazak Kinder, Inc.,
No. 21-2883, 2023 U.S. Dist. LEXIS 168647
(E.D.N.Y. Sept. 21, 2023)....256

Johnson v. Maraj,
No. 23-5061, 2023 U.S. Dist. LEXIS 230527
(C.D. Cal. Dec. 15, 2023)....243

Johnston v. Kroeger,
No. 23-5024, 2024 U.S. App. LEXIS 3806
(5th Cir. Feb. 19, 2024)....281, 283

Jones v. Atl. Records,
No. 22-893, 2023 U.S. Dist. LEXIS 152283
(S.D.N.Y. Aug. 29, 2023)....302

Kadrey v. Meta Platforms, Inc.,
No. 23-3417, 2023 U.S. Dist. LEXIS 207683
(N.D. Cal. Nov. 20, 2023)....303

Kerson v. Vermont Law School,
79 F.4th 257
(2d Cir. 2023)....352

Kreatio Software Priv. Ltd. v. IDG Commc'ns, Inc.,
No. 23-10273, 2024 U.S. Dist. LEXIS 51279
(D. Mass. Mar. 22, 2024)....247

Kremer v. Alphabet Inc.,
No. 23-52, 2024 U.S. Dist. LEXIS 37138
(M.D. Tenn. Mar. 4, 2024)....236

Laatz v. Zazzle, Inc.,
682 F. Supp. 3d 791
(N.D. Cal. 2023)....343

Laatz v. Zazzle, Inc.,
No. 22-4844, 2024 U.S. Dist. LEXIS 40600
(N.D. Cal. Mar. 7, 2024)....277

Laatz v. Zazzle, Inc.,
No. 22-4844, 2024 U.S. Dist. LEXIS 4838
(N.D. Cal. Jan. 9, 2024)....260

Lane Coder Photography, LLC v. Hearst Corp.,
No. 22-5071, 2023 U.S. Dist. LEXIS 159200
(S.D.N.Y. Sept. 8, 2023)....296, 302, 347

Lee v. Warner Media, LLC,
No. 23-6025, 2023 U.S. Dist. LEXIS 211437
(W.D.N.Y. Nov. 28, 2023)....286

LeSEA, Inc. v. LeSEA Broad. Corp.,
No. 18-914, 2023 U.S. Dist. LEXIS 148026
(N.D. Ind. Aug. 22, 2023)....320

Live Face on Web, LLC v. Cremation Soc'y of Ill., Inc.,
77 F.4th 630
(7th Cir. 2023)....328

Livingston v. Jay Livingston Music, Inc.,
No. 22-532, 2024 U.S. Dist. LEXIS 29398
(M.D. Tenn. Feb. 21, 2024)....264

Loeb-Defever v. Mako, L.L.C.,
No. 22-20362, 2023 U.S. App. LEXIS 23004
(5th Cir. Aug. 30, 2023)....267, 346

Lowery v. Rhapsody Int'l, Inc.,
75 F.4th 985
(9th Cir. 2023)....326

Markham Concepts v. Hasbro, Inc.,
71 F.4th 80
(1st Cir. 2023)....328

McFee v. Carolina Pad, LLC,
No. 21-633, 2023 U.S. Dist. LEXIS 205753
(W.D.N.C. Nov. 16, 2023) 293

McGlynn v. Sinovision Inc.,
No. 23-4826, 2024 U.S. Dist. LEXIS 26641
(S.D.N.Y. Feb. 15, 2024) 315

Merrill v. Hyman,
No. 22-2971, 2024 U.S. App. LEXIS 1140
(2d Cir. Jan. 18, 2024) 262

Minden Pictures Inc. v. Ammoland, Inc.,
No. 20-2276, 2023 U.S. Dist. LEXIS 113697
(D.N.J. June 30, 2023) 250

MMAS Rsch., LLC v. Charite,
No. 23-55202, 2024 U.S. App. LEXIS 6004
(9th Cir. Mar. 13, 2024) 250

Moss v. Miller,
No. 23-7424, 2023 U.S. Dist. LEXIS 226013
(C.D. Cal. Dec. 15, 2023) 263, 317

Nat'l Presto Indus. v. United States Merchs. Fin. Grp., Inc.,
No. 18-3321, 2023 U.S. Dist. LEXIS 206092
(D. Minn. Nov. 17, 2023) 325, 340

NEO4J, Inc. v. Purethink, LLC,
No. 18-7182, 2023 U.S. Dist. LEXIS 191809
(N.D. Cal. Oct. 25, 2023) 338, 348

Neu Productions Inc. v. Outside Interactive, Inc.,
No. 23-4125, 2024 U.S. Dist. LEXIS 47842
(S.D.N.Y. Mar. 19, 2024) 241, 342

New Directions Program v. Sierra Health & Wellness Ctrs. LLC,
No. 22-1090, 2023 U.S. Dist. LEXIS 196561
(E.D. Cal. Nov. 1, 2023) 244

Niehuss v. Colossal Biosciences, Inc.,
No. 20-617, 2023 U.S.Dist. LEXIS 210071
(W.D. Tex. Nov. 27, 2023) 247

Norris v. Goldner,
No. 19-5491, 2023 U.S. Dist. LEXIS 151689
(S.D.N.Y. Aug. 24, 2023) 268

Okolita v. Amazon.com, Inc.,
No. 22-284, 2023 U.S. Dist. LEXIS 130477
(D. Me. July 28, 2023) 301

Oliver v. Meow Wolf, Inc.,
No. 20-237, 2023 U.S. Dist. LEXIS 104919
(D.N.M. June 16, 2023) 272

Oliver v. Meow Wolf, Inc.,
No. 20-237, 2023 U.S. Dist. LEXIS 114812
(D.N.M. July 5, 2023) 280

Patrick v. Poree,
No. 23-12732, 2023 U.S. App. LEXIS 33078
(11th Cir. Dec. 14, 2023) 262

Paulo v. Agence France Presse,
No. 21-11209, 2023 U.S. Dist. LEXIS 207171
(S.D.N.Y. Oct. 17, 2023) 238, 330

Peabody & Co. LLC v. Wayne,
No. 22-10316, 2024 U.S. Dist. LEXIS 24268
(S.D.N.Y. Feb. 12, 2024) 285

Petro. Serv. Co. v. Santie's Wholesale Oil Co.,
No. 23-1500, 2024 U.S. Dist. LEXIS 33401
(M.D. Pa. Feb. 27, 2024) 239

Philpot v. Indep. J. Review,
92 F.4th 252
(4th Cir. 2024) 275, 308

Polychron v. Bezos,
No. 23-2831, 2023 U.S. Dist. LEXIS 226148
(C.D. Cal. Dec. 14, 2023) 332

Poppington, LLC v. Brooks,
No. 23-660, 2024 U.S. App. LEXIS 7112
(2d Cir. Mar. 26, 2024) 325

Premier Dealer Servs., Inc. v. Allegiance Adm'rs, LLC,
93 F.4th 985
(6th Cir. 2024) 254

Ragan v. Berkshire Hathaway Auto., Inc.,
91 F.4th 1267
(8th Cir. 2024) 255

Reiffer v. NYC Luxury Limousine Ltd.,
No. 22-2374, 2023 U.S. Dist. LEXIS 104552
(S.D.N.Y. June 15, 2023) 324, 331

Richardson v. Kharbouch,
No. 19-2321, 2024 U.S. Dist. LEXIS 1815
(N.D. Ill. Jan. 4, 2024) 279

Roadget Bus. PTE. LTD v. PDD Holdings Inc.,
No. 22-07119, 2023 U.S. Dist. LEXIS 131974
(N.D. Ill. July 31, 2023) 350

Ronk v. Hudson,
No. 20-9843, 2023 U.S. Dist. LEXIS 204089
(C.D. Cal. Nov. 13, 2023) 282

Roskovensky v. Sanibel Captiva Island Vacation Rentals, LLC,
No. 22-602, 2024 U.S. Dist. LEXIS 45778
(M.D. Fla. Mar. 15, 2024) 270

Russell v. Walmart Inc.,
No. 19-5495, 2023 U.S. Dist. LEXIS 151712
(C.D. Cal. Aug. 17, 2023) 304

Russell v. Walmart Inc.,
No. 19-5495, 2024 U.S. Dist. LEXIS 15631
(C.D. Cal. Jan. 2, 2024) 332

Sadowski v. Site Spin Off. LLC,
No. 23-297, 2023 U.S. Dist. LEXIS 124329
(M.D. Fla. July 19, 2023) 231

Seventh Chakra Films, LLC v. Alesse,
No. 21-21286, 2023 U.S. Dist. LEXIS 185481
(S.D. Fla. Oct. 15, 2023) 334

Shande v. Zoox, Inc.,
No. 22-5821, 2023 U.S. Dist. LEXIS 141606
(N.D. Cal. Aug. 14, 2023) 349

Simpson Strong-Tie Co. v. MiTek Inc.,
No. 20-6957, 2023 U.S. Dist. LEXIS 223876
(N.D. Cal. Dec. 15, 2023) 256, 288

Softketeers, Inc. v. Regal West Corp.,
No. 19-519, 2023 U.S. Dist. LEXIS 233249
(C.D. Cal. Dec. 26, 2023) 261, 265, 270

Sony Music En., Inc. v. Cox Communs., Inc.,
93 F.4th 222
(4th Cir. 2024) 295

Sony Music Ent., Inc. v. Clark-Rainbolt,
No. 23-275, 2024 U.S. Dist. LEXIS 54798
(N.D. Tex. Mar. 27, 2024) 338

Sound & Color, LLC v. Smith,
No. 22-1508, 2023 U.S. Dist. LEXIS 158043
(C.D. Cal. Sept. 6, 2023) 289

State Street Global Advisors Tr. Co. v. Visbal,
677 F. Supp. 3d 209
(S.D.N.Y. 2023) 286, 295

Stebbins v. Google LLC,
No. 23-322, 2023 U.S. Dist. LEXIS 169937
(N.D. Cal. Aug. 31, 2023) 309
Stokes v. Brinor, Inc.,
No. 22-973, 2023 U.S. Dist. LEXIS 123840
(N.D. Ohio July 18, 2023) 305, 320
Stringer v. Richard,
No. 21-632, 2023 U.S. Dist. LEXIS 122818
(N.D. Ohio Jul. 17, 2023) 335
Tecnoglass LLC v. Paredes,
No. 22- 22356, 2023 U.S. Dist. LEXIS 116974
(S.D. Fla. July 6, 2023) 291, 339
Thaler v. Perlmutter,
No. 22-1564, 2023 U.S. Dist. LEXIS 145823
(D.D.C. Aug. 18, 2023) 257, 278
That One Video Ent. LLC v. Koil Content Creation Pty Ltd.,
No. 23-2687, 2024 U.S. Dist. LEXIS 27005
(C.D. Cal. Feb. 14, 2024) 265
Thiccc Boy Prod. v. Swindelles,
No. 22-90, 2024 U.S. Dist. LEXIS 30287
(D.R.I. Feb. 22, 2024) 312
Thomson Reuters Enter. Ctr. GmbH v. Ross Intel. Inc.,
No. 20-613, 2023 U.S. Dist. LEXIS 170155
(D. Del. Sept. 25, 2023) 292, 301, 313
Thumbtack, Inc. v. Liaison, Inc.,
No. 23-2830, 2024 U.S. Dist. LEXIS 11022
(N.D. Cal. Jan. 22, 2024) 256
Tolkien Tr. v. Polychron,
No. 23-4300, 2023 U.S. Dist. LEXIS 226135
(C.D. Cal. Dec. 14, 2023) 288, 337
Tomelleri v. SunFrog, LLC,
No. 23-10370, 2024 U.S. Dist. LEXIS 38378
(E.D. Mich. Mar. 5, 2024) 248
Topalsson GmbH v. Bayerische Motoren Werke AG,
No. 23-1823, 2023 U.S. Dist. LEXIS 190229
(C.D. Cal. Oct. 23, 2023) 238
Tremblay v. OpenAI, Inc.,
Nos. 23-3223, 23-3416, 2024 U.S. Dist. LEXIS 24618
(N.D. Cal. Feb. 12, 2024) 297, 348
Trendtex Fabrics, Ltd. v. Bonnie Brown Designs, Inc.,
No. 23-20291, 2023 U.S. Dist. LEXIS 126598
(S.D. Fla. July 21, 2023) 248, 250, 252

Trent P. Fisher Enters., LLC v. SAS Automation, LLC,
No. 20-216, 2023 U.S. Dist. LEXIS 135933
(S.D. Ohio Aug. 3, 2023) 272, 274, 321, 325, 350

UIRC-GSA Holdings, LLC v. William Blair & Co., L.L.C.,
90 F.4th 908
(7th Cir. 2024) 254

UIRC-GSA Holdings, LLC v. William Blair & Co., L.L.C.,
Nos. 23-1527, 23-2566, 2024 U.S. App. LEXIS 6500
(7th Cir. Mar. 19, 2024) 327

UMG Recordings, Inc. v. Internet Archive,
No. 23-7133, 2023 U.S. Dist. LEXIS 219243
(S.D.N.Y. Dec. 8, 2023) 237

Universal Prot. Serv. v. Coastal Fire & Integration Sys., Inc.,
No. 22-1352, 2023 U.S. Dist. LEXIS 104689
(S.D. Cal. June 15, 2023) 245

Uworld LLC v. Usmle Galaxy LLC,
No. 23-447, 2023 U.S. Dist. LEXIS 119673
(N.D. Tex. June 27, 2023) 344

Valancourt Books, LLC v. Garland,
82 F.4th 1222
(D.C. Cir. 2023) 273

Versluys v. Weizenbaum,
No. 21-1694, 2024 U.S. Dist. LEXIS 38364
(D. Or. Mar. 4, 2024) 336

VidAngel LLC v. ClearPlay, Inc.,
No. 14-160, 2023 U.S. Dist. LEXIS 207970
(D. Utah Nov. 20, 2023) 351

Wanjuan Media (Tianjin) Co., Ltd. v. Amazon.Com, Inc.,
No. 22-1434, 2024 U.S. Dist. LEXIS 41209
(S.D.N.Y. Mar. 8, 2024) 267, 315

Warner Chappell Music, Inc. v. Nealy,
No. 22-1078, 601 U.S. ___
(2024) 322

We the Protesters, Inc. v. Sinyangwe,
No. 22-9565, 2024 U.S. Dist. LEXIS 49532
(S.D.N.Y. Mar. 20, 2024) 241, 346

Whyte Monkee Prods., LLC v. Netflix, Inc.,
97 F.4th 699
(10th Cir. 2024) 306

Widespread Elec. Sales, LLC v. Upstate Breaker Wholesale Supply, Inc.,
No. 20-2541, 2023 U.S. Dist. LEXIS 224054
(N.D. Tex. Dec. 17, 2023) 258, 290

Wilder v. Hoiland,
No. 22-1254, 2024 U.S. Dist. LEXIS 18051
(S.D.N.Y. Feb. 1, 2024) 273, 309

Williams v. Bobo,
No. 22-3561, 2023 U.S. Dist. LEXIS 128798
(S.D. Ohio July 25, 2023) 319

Williams v. D'Youville Coll.,
No. 21-1001, 2024 U.S. Dist. LEXIS 23979
(W.D.N.Y. Feb. 9, 2024) 269

Wozniak v. Warner Bros. Ent. Inc.,
No. 22-8969, 2024 U.S. Dist. LEXIS 55146
(S.D.N.Y. Mar. 27, 2024) 276, 283

I. JURISDICTION AND PROCEDURAL ISSUES

A. Subject Matter Jurisdiction

Kremer v. Alphabet Inc., No. 23-52, 2024 U.S. Dist. LEXIS 37138 (M.D. Tenn. Mar. 4, 2024)

Magistrate recommended defendant's motion to dismiss be granted and that court dismiss action under Rule 12(b)(6) for failure to state claim on which relief can be granted. *Pro se* plaintiff small business owner sued defendant Alphabet (parent company of Google). Plaintiff alleged Google displayed his "registered copyright image" without his approval and asserted claims of copyright infringement. Complaint's caption named only Google, but plaintiff used term "Defendant" interchangeably to describe Google and Alphabet. He attached certificate of registration from Copyright Office for photograph titled "Maxwell kremer's image 3." Alphabet removed to federal court and moved to dismiss plaintiff's complaint, arguing lack of subject matter jurisdiction and that plaintiff's claims were "wholly unsubstantial, if not fantastical, and devoid of merit." Magistrate first recommended Alphabet's motion to dismiss based on lack of subject matter jurisdiction be denied. Federal copyright law and plaintiff's copyright claims provided basis for court's jurisdiction. Defendant failed to show plaintiff's allegations entirely without foundation—its only jurisdictional argument was that plaintiff's copyright claims were based solely on his photo appearing in search results with no infringement analysis. However, Alphabet did not address fact that plaintiff submitted certificate of registration stating he was author and copyright claimant of image in question. Magistrate next recommended dismissal of action under Rule 12(b)(6) for failure to state claim. Plaintiff alleged Google's search engine displayed his registered copyright image without his approval but failed to allege any specific wrongdoing by Alphabet, and thereby failed to establish Alphabet's plausible liability for Google's actions.

B. Personal Jurisdiction and Venue

Davis v. ABC, No. 22-5944, 2024 U.S. Dist. LEXIS 48187 (S.D.N.Y. Mar. 19, 2024)

District court denied without prejudice defendants' motions to dismiss second amended complaint for lack of personal jurisdiction. Plaintiff public school teacher and writer authored television script *This School Year* ("*TSY*") based on personal experience as teacher. In March 2020, plaintiff registered *TSY* with Copyright Office. Mid-2020, plaintiff began working with defendant production company and individual Cherisse Parks (together with production company, "BPP

Defendants") to bring *TSY* to market, including signing NDA and corresponding about script. Plaintiff was told BPP Defendants would help present *TSY* to major outlets such as Hulu and ABC. BPP Defendants gave plaintiff notes on script, which plaintiff incorporated, but at some point during 2020 BPP Defendants stopped responding. Show *Abbott Elementary* was pitched to ABC by actor Quinta Brunson (together, "Abbott Defendants" along with other individuals connected to show) in late 2020, and pilot aired following year. Court found plaintiff successfully pleaded personal jurisdiction over BPP Defendants. Three requirements under New York law are: (1) plaintiff's service of process must be proper, (2) must be statutory basis for personal jurisdiction that renders service effective, and (3) exercise of personal jurisdiction must comport with constitutional due process principles. Court analyzed CPLR provision plaintiff pointed to governing non-domiciliary who transacts business within state. Here, plaintiff lived in New York and engaged in email correspondence with BPP, through which she received BPP nondisclosure agreement that she signed and returned in and from New York. Plaintiff sent copies of *TSY* to BPP from New York. She had at least one call with BPP while plaintiff was in New York. Court found it was evident that alleged claims of infringement arose from BPP's business transactions with plaintiff, through individual Parks, given causal connection between execution of NDA and plaintiff's provision of allegedly infringed work to BPP. Court weighed traditional notions of fair play and substantial justice and found preliminary exercise of personal jurisdiction over Parks and BPP Defendants would not offend such notions. Court therefore denied motion to dismiss due to lack of personal jurisdiction.

UMG Recordings, Inc. v. Internet Archive, No. 23-7133, 2023 U.S. Dist. LEXIS 219243 (S.D.N.Y. Dec. 8, 2023)

District court granted defendants' motion to transfer venue to Northern District of California. Plaintiff companies were involved in production, manufacture, and sale of sound recordings. Complaint alleged infringement of plaintiffs' copyrights in recordings on 78 rpm records. Defendants digitized and uploaded plaintiffs' recordings as part of Internet Archive's Great 78 Project. Collectors of 78 rpm records could deliver physical records to non-profit Internet Archive's headquarters in San Francisco, where they were sent to Pennsylvania for digitization. Digital versions were uploaded in California and stored on servers there. Plaintiffs filed suit in Southern District of New York, and defendants moved to transfer venue to Northern District of California. Court weighed *forum non conveniens* factors. Convenience of witnesses considered most important factor, and obvious and primary witnesses with information about alleged infringement were defendants themselves or employees of Internet Archive, located in California. Another important factor, location of relevant documents and ease of access to proof, weighed slightly in favor of transfer because relevant documentary evidence and allegedly infringing digital archives likely to be kept by Internet Archive in San Francisco. Locus of operative facts was primary factor in court's decision: Internet Archive headquartered in San Francisco and other defendants also based there; servers hosting 78 Project's website were in California; business arrangement between defendants established at Internet Archive's California headquarters; digital files sent from Pennsylvania to California, where they were uploaded to Project's website; and some physical 78 rpm records were stored in California. Nexus between New York and operative facts more tenuous—Project website accessed by some New York users. Weighing all factors, court granted transfer of venue.

Paulo v. Agence France Presse, No. 21-11209, 2023 U.S. Dist. LEXIS 207171 (S.D.N.Y. Oct. 17, 2023)

Magistrate judge recommended denial of defendants' motion for attorneys' fees and costs. Portuguese photojournalist Leong Francisco Paulo sued Agence France Presse (AFP) and two Getty Images corporate entities for infringement and violations of CMI. Related litigation also commenced in Portuguese court. District court conditionally dismissed claims filed in Southern District of New York based on *forum non conveniens* and lack of personal jurisdiction, on condition that defendants agree to submit to jurisdiction of Portuguese court. On motion for fees and costs, magistrate concluded that dismissal for *forum non conveniens* did not establish defendants as prevailing parties, necessary condition to obtain attorneys' fees and costs. Dismissal for lack of personal jurisdiction also did not transform defendants into prevailing parties, because decision did not insulate defendants from risk of future litigation; indeed, condition of dismissal was that plaintiff remained free to bring claims against AFP in Portugal. Defendants therefore failed to establish necessary condition of prevailing party. Defendants also sought costs under 28 U.S.C. § 1919, which allows for award of costs when dismissal is for lack of jurisdiction. However, district court noted that dismissal on *forum non conveniens* grounds does not constitute lack of jurisdiction. Though dismissal for lack of personal jurisdiction could allow for costs under § 1919, district court concluded that discretionary factors weighed against awarding costs. Finally, though Rule 41(d)(1) allows for fees incurred when plaintiff dismisses action and then refiles against same defendant, district court held that Rule 41(d)(1) applies to litigation within United States that was previously dismissed by plaintiff, not extraterritorial litigation.

Topalsson GmbH v. Bayerische Motoren Werke AG, No. 23-1823, 2023 U.S. Dist. LEXIS 190229 (C.D. Cal. Oct. 23, 2023)

District court granted in part and denied in part defendants' motion to dismiss amended complaint for lack personal jurisdiction and *forum non conveniens*. German corporate plaintiff, creator of customizable images of vehicle configurations, alleged that defendant auto manufacturers had infringed four copyrights that plaintiff owned in connection with its software programs. In October 2019, plaintiff entered into service agreement with non-party Rolls-Royce Motor Cars Ltd. to develop software for 2020 Rolls-Royce vehicle. In

March 2020, defendants hired plaintiff's competitor for same project and then terminated services agreement with plaintiff. Prior to filing suit in this case, plaintiff and Rolls-Royce litigated claims in UK relating to alleged breach of service agreement. Exclusive jurisdiction clause within agreement between plaintiff and Rolls-Royce stated that each party agreed to submit to exclusive jurisdiction of Courts of England and Wales; agreement stated it was for benefit of Rolls-Royce and any relevant BMW Group entities. District court determined that forum selection clause applied to defendant BMW Group and Rolls-Royce's distributor in North America, because both entities were affiliated with and closely related to Rolls-Royce. Dealership defendants, however, were independent of Rolls-Royce and its corporate affiliates. District court therefore granted motion to dismiss with respect to BMW Group and Rolls-Royce's distributor in North America, and denied motion with respect to independent dealer defendants. Regarding *forum non conveniens* factors, and applying them only to BMW Group and Rolls-Royce's North American distributor, district court found adequate foreign forum existed for such defendants. In addition, public interest favored dismissal because nearly all alleged conduct related to copyright infringement occurring through technology of parties located outside United States. District court declined to address personal jurisdiction argument of BMW Group defendant due to partial dismissal on grounds of *forum non conveniens*.

Petro. Serv. Co. v. Santie's Wholesale Oil Co., No. 23-1500, 2024 U.S. Dist. LEXIS 33401 (M.D. Pa. Feb. 27, 2024)

Plaintiff distributor of oil and lubricants, based in Pennsylvania, sued for infringement in Middle District of Pennsylvania alleging defendant copied and created derivative works of its copyrighted website containing "various propriety images and descriptions of branded products"; defendant moved to transfer venue to its home venue of Eastern District of Missouri. On motion to transfer, Pennsylvania district court agreed with defendant that Act provides for suit to be brought "in the district in which the defendant or his agent resides or may be found," and then turned to remaining private and public interest factors on propriety of transfer. Considering private interest factors, district court credited defendant's argument that allegedly infringing conduct occurred in Missouri (where defendant is located and seeking to transfer case), and largely rejected plaintiff's argument that infringement took place on defendant's website and thus "arose wherever the internet may be freely accessed." District court further discounted plaintiff's argument that plaintiff suffered "harm" in Pennsylvania, instead favoring defendant's argument that "alleged harm to plaintiff originated in Missouri," source of alleged infringement. District court found remaining private interest factors (relating to convenience to parties in producing witnesses and books and records) neutral, since both parties are required to produce witnesses, and books and records at issued are stored electronically and thus easy to transfer. On public interest factors (relating to where litigation can proceed "in the most efficient and inexpensive fashion"), defendant relied on data from "statistical comparisons between the Eastern District of Missouri and the Middle District of Pennsylvania using caseload data from the Administrative Office of United States Courts" in arguing that Eastern District of Missouri had greater judicial resources available, and on average disposed of cases more quickly, than Middle District of Pennsylvania. Considering all factors, district court found defendant met burden in demonstrating its preferred forum was more favorable, and granted motion to transfer venue.

Dermansky v. Young Turks, Inc., No. 22-345, 2023 U.S. Dist. LEXIS 114797 (D. Del. July 5, 2023)

District court granted defendant's motion to transfer venue from District of Delaware to Central District of California. In granting motion, court weighed number of factors. Neither party resided in Delaware. Defendant, online media company, was incorporated in Delaware but domiciled in California. Meanwhile, plaintiff, photographer, resided in Louisiana and was not otherwise connected to Delaware. Claim of alleged infringement arose in California at defendant's headquarters. Plaintiff argued its preference not to travel to California from Louisiana due to Covid-19, as Delaware is closer to Louisiana, but had also filed and litigated other infringement suits in California during pandemic, undercutting its argument. California was location of defendant's witnesses, books and records in relation to alleged infringement (though that factor given little weight by court due to technological advances). Volume of filings in California court was lesser than volume of filings in Delaware court, so less administrative burden for courts if venue transferred to California. Finally, as defendant was media company and plaintiff was photographer in media industry, court determined that California, as one of world's entertainment capitals, had more local interest in deciding controversy. Court found that factors weighed in favor of transferring venue from Delaware to California.

Fernandez v. Jagger, No. 23-891, 2023 U.S. Dist. LEXIS 186839 (E.D. La. Oct. 17, 2023)

District court granted defendant's motion to dismiss for improper venue. Plaintiff, songwriter, alleged copyright infringement by defendants Mick Jagger and Keith Richards and affiliated publisher BMG and distributor UMG, claiming 2020 Rolling Stones song "Living in a Ghost Town" featured "recognizable and key protected elements" of two songs by plaintiff. Plaintiff filed suit in Eastern District of Louisiana, and defendants filed motion to dismiss for improper venue, arguing that none of defendants resided or were domiciled in District, nor were they subject to personal jurisdiction in District. Plaintiff argued that venue in District was proper because defendants were "in the business of selling and distributing their musical works worldwide" and "purposely availed themselves to Louisiana by placing their works into the stream of commerce." Court sided with defendants, finding that none of defendants resided or were domiciled in District, as Jagger and Richards were UK citizens with no District residence and

Rolling Stones only performed in District four times in decades (and such performances were before release of "Living in a Ghost Town"); meanwhile, defendants BMG and UMG were incorporated and had principal offices in other states, not District. Court addressed plaintiff's argument that defendants directed activities to District, finding any such connection to be "highly attenuated." Accordingly, court agreed that venue in District was improper and granted motion to dismiss.

C. Pleadings

Neu Productions Inc. v. Outside Interactive, Inc., No. 23-4125, 2024 U.S. Dist. LEXIS 47842 (S.D.N.Y. Mar. 19, 2024)

Magistrate judge recommended granting motion to dismiss copyright claims in part but allowing repleading to cure fact that complaint was filed before certain registrations had been obtained. Plaintiff film production company created programs for defendant, operator of outdoors-themed television channels and streaming services. Plaintiffs filmed 16 episodes of television series and licensed them to defendant for use on its television channel for limited time pursuant to what parties agreed was implied license. Plaintiffs licensed additional show to defendant in perpetuity. Plaintiffs alleged that defendant expanded its use of plaintiffs' content beyond defendant's television channel and onto defendant's streaming service, exceeding scope of parties' agreements. Plaintiffs filed infringement claim against defendant's expanded use. Because plaintiffs' allegations must be taken as true, and there was no written license to disprove plaintiff's assertions, court denied motion to dismiss infringement claim. Defendant also moved to dismiss certain copyrights for which plaintiff did not obtain registrations until after complaint was filed, but court granted leave for plaintiff to amend complaint so that operative pleading could postdate all relevant registrations, finding that no prejudice would ensue from amendment when discovery had not yet begun.

We the Protesters, Inc. v. Sinyangwe, No. 22-9565, 2024 U.S. Dist. LEXIS 49532 (S.D.N.Y. Mar. 20, 2024)

District court denied plaintiffs' motion to dismiss infringement counterclaim, finding defendants properly alleged ownership of valid copyright and copying of constituent elements of work that are original, and granted plaintiffs' motion to dismiss DMCA counterclaim only as to modified website. Defendants created website that collected and assembled information on reported incidents of police violence across country. Plaintiffs entered into collaboration with defendants. Defendants alleged that plaintiffs attempted to gain access to defendants' account to access or edit website, and after failed attempt, published copycat version of website. Court determined defendants did not need to assert exactly which individual elements of copyrighted works were infringed at motion to dismiss stage. Court found concept of websites, mapping incidents of police killings, undoubtedly similar, but had doubts over proposition that protectible aspects of website were substantially similar to those in plaintiffs'. Court found plaintiffs' arguments attacking defendants' selection, coordination, and arrangement theory unavailing because fact that plaintiffs were unable to accurately update database allegedly copied does not mean plaintiffs did not copy database in first instance. Court also found unavailing plaintiff's argument that police killings data constituted basic facts not copyrightable because argument failed to take into account that defendants' copyright claim concerned selection, coordination, and arrangement of those facts and not facts themselves. Court found website passed originality test because defendants used color choices and picked certain graphics with specific goal in mind. Plaintiffs also moved to dismiss DMCA counterclaim which alleges plaintiffs violated DMCA's prohibition on removing CMI from website. Court granted plaintiffs' motion to dismiss counterclaim inasmuch as claim was predicated on plaintiffs' modified website because website and plaintiffs' modified website distinct. However, website and plaintiffs' original website were at least close to identical so court at motion to dismiss stage allowed counterclaim to proceed only on basis of pre-modified version of website.

nKlosures, Inc. Architects v. Avalon Lodging, LLC, No. 22-459, 2024 U.S. Dist. LEXIS 54274 (C.D. Cal. Mar. 25, 2024)

District court granted in part and denied in part defendant's motion for judgment on pleadings. Plaintiff architectural firm alleged defendant hotel developer infringed plaintiff's architectural designs. Plaintiff and defendant's predecessor-in-interest Patel entered into agreement for works to be implemented into hotel design and development ("Project"). When Patel sold interest in Project to defendant, plaintiff and defendant discussed works and plaintiff confirmed works could only continue to be used for Project if defendant paid plaintiff, to which defendant generally agreed. However, afterwards, defendant ceased all contact with plaintiff and proceeded to promote Project in connection with written plans for works. Plaintiff alleged infringement and sought attorneys' fees and statutory damages. Defendant moved for judgment on pleadings, arguing plaintiff failed to allege with particularity which portions of works were infringed, and how defendant was vicariously liable for infringement, given defendant lacked ability to implement architectural plans. Defendant argued further that plaintiff was not entitled to fees or statutory damages due to plaintiff's failure to register works prior to alleged infringement or within three months after first publication of works, which plaintiff conceded. Accordingly, district court granted in part defendant's motion for judgment on pleadings as to defendant's claims regarding attorneys' fees and statutory damages. However, district court denied defendant's motion as to defendant's claims regarding plaintiff's failure to allege infringement with particularity, finding plaintiff "adequately pled its claim for copyright infringement at this stage by alleging its ownership of the drawings and plans, its registration of the copyright, and the infringement by [defendant]."

BMG Rts. Mgmt. (United States) LLC v. Joyy Inc., No. 22-1578, 2024 U.S. Dist. LEXIS 25438 (C.D. Cal. Feb. 12, 2024)

District court granted defendants' motion to dismiss direct infringement claim because plaintiff failed to allege volitional conduct. Defendants, technology companies, operated Likee, social media platform based on user-generated short video content similar to TikTok. Plaintiff, music publisher and record label, sued defendants, for direct copyright infringement on grounds that defendants allowed users to upload or link to personal music libraries, that Likee app copied underlying copyrighted material and published copy on app, that defendants encouraged and facilitated infringement by their creators, and that defendants stored, curated, reproduced and distributed plaintiff's music without authorization. Court found that plaintiff had failed to establish necessary causal nexus between defendants' conduct and their users' illegal copying. Automatic copying, storing or transmission or copyrighted material by website owners like defendants was insufficient to allege volitional conduct by defendants. Moreover, plaintiff did not allege that defendants had selected any material for, or had themselves culled copyright works for, upload, download, transmission or storage. Nor did defendants exercise control other than by general operation of Likee, which did not constitute intervening act giving rise to volitional conduct. Finally, plaintiff did not allege that defendants had instigated copying, storage or distribution of copyrighted materials. Because plaintiff failed to allege volitional conduct, it had failed to state direct copyright infringement claim.

Johnson v. Maraj, No. 23-5061, 2023 U.S. Dist. LEXIS 230527 (C.D. Cal. Dec. 15, 2023)

District court dismissed plaintiff's direct, vicarious and contributory infringement claims where he failed to plead facts to plausibly allege substantial similarity between songs at issue. Plaintiff musician and composer alleged he created musical work "OnMySleeve" ("Work") before attending Art Institute of Atlanta from 2012 to 2015. First Amended Complaint ("FAC") alleged that defendant music artists, producers, and publishers—including associates of Nicki Minaj and Michael Williams—were present at or attended Institute during same time. Plaintiff alleged that following recording session in audio production studio, his hard drive containing Work was taken and that defendants had access to studio. Plaintiff further alleged defendants copied his sound recording and/or musical composition of his Work, then created and distributed infringing work "I Lied," which appeared on Minaj's album and Williams' mixtape. Before bringing suit, plaintiff obtained copyright registration for sound recording of Work. After commencing action, plaintiff filed application for supplementary registration of musical composition of Work. Court found that, while plaintiff owned valid copyright registration for sound recording, he did not own one for musical composition. Merely filing application was not sufficient to plausibly allege ownership, so, to extent plaintiff alleged defendants infringed musical composition, plaintiff failed to state claim for copyright infringement. Court next discussed requirement to plead facts plausibly showing either that works in question are strikingly similar or substantially similar and that defendants had access. Here, FAC failed to plead facts to plausibly allege that Work and "I Lied" were substantially or strikingly similar. FAC instead contained conclusory allegations, and plaintiff failed to allege protectible elements of Work that were strikingly or substantially similar to "I Lied." Plaintiff therefore failed to state claim for copyright infringement. Accordingly, court also dismissed plaintiff's claims for vicarious and contributory infringement.

New Directions Program v. Sierra Health & Wellness Ctrs. LLC, No. 22-1090, 2023 U.S. Dist. LEXIS 196561 (E.D. Cal. Nov. 1, 2023)

District court granted defendants' motion to dismiss copyright infringement claim as to book, but denied as to DVD and brochure. Plaintiffs developed outpatient treatment model and authored book on subject. Plaintiffs alleged defendants used and published copies of portions of book, including copying and using treatment documents with clients; that defendants sold DVD and booklet that copied parts of book; and that defendants offered brochure that copied portions of book. Court found plaintiffs did not allege facts indicating original work or part of original work copied by defendants. Plaintiffs did not allege any details regarding which treatment documents and portions of book were copied. Similarly, court found plaintiffs failed to allege that defendants unlawfully appropriated work. Court granted motion to dismiss infringement claim arising from copying portions of book and treatment documents. Court found plaintiffs showed facts of significant overlap allowing court to draw reasonable inference that topics discussed in book and topics presented in DVD were not created independently. Court found plaintiffs alleged objective similarities, such that both book and DVD included lists of topics explored with same wording. Court denied motion to dismiss infringement claim arising from DVD. Court found plaintiffs sufficiently alleged copying as to brochure because defendants had access to book and used verbatim same six stages of recovery, and accordingly denied motion to dismiss infringement claim arising from brochure.

August Image, LLC v. Trend Hunter Inc., No. 22-7120, 2023 U.S. Dist. LEXIS 162807 (C.D. Cal. Sept. 12, 2023)

District court denied defendant's motion to dismiss copyright infringement claim, finding plaintiff sufficiently stated claims. Plaintiff, licensing agent of photographers, sued defendant for infringement arising from defendant's use of photographs taken by photographers, which were allegedly reproduced, distributed, and publicly displayed on defendant's website without authorization or payment. Defendant argued plaintiff's claim was impermissibly vague and failed to adequately specify which works allegedly infringed. Court found plaintiff's claims sufficiently pled because plaintiff alleged ownership of copyrights, registration, and copying by defendant posting photographs on website. Court found plaintiff adequately alleged defendant may be liable for contributory or vicarious infringement because plaintiff alleged defendant's founder repeatedly failed to obtain proper clearances and licenses despite being sophisticated publisher, and defendant financially benefitted from infringing activity.

Universal Prot. Serv. v. Coastal Fire & Integration Sys., Inc., No. 22-1352, 2023 U.S. Dist. LEXIS 104689 (S.D. Cal. June 15, 2023)

Court granted in part and denied in part plaintiffs' motion to dismiss infringement claims against defendants for use of custom AutoCAD templates and Quote Builder tool. Plaintiffs' security services company provided video surveillance, alarm monitoring, etc. and owned several copyrights to assist with engineering designs and estimates: two AutoCAD templates and Quote Builder. AutoCAD technical drawings included symbols, formats, illustrations, layouts, etc. unique to plaintiff. Plaintiffs acquired another security services company. Plaintiffs alleged that during time of their employment, two individuals who came from acquired company directly competed with plaintiffs through their own company (additional named defendant) by doing exact or similar nature of what they did for plaintiffs. In June 2022, plaintiffs received bid to install security system, and defendant company's design drawing was attached bearing one of individual defendants' initials. Plaintiffs alleged design drawing infringed on its AutoCAD technical drawings. Court found plaintiffs sufficiently alleged cognizable claim for infringement of technical drawings. First, plaintiffs demonstrated ownership of copyrighted work. Second, plaintiffs alleged use of works by alleging defendants had access to templates during their employment and that there were substantial similarities between drawings and allegedly infringing design. Defendants argued templates were computer programs, and only way to infringe would have been by creating new version of existing program, not drawing. Court disagreed, pointing out AutoCAD templates are not software programs, but custom drawings that store default styles, settings, and layouts, and serve as starting point for creating drawings. Court cited similar case where copying was found where defendant used copyrighted template to create allegedly infringing reports, where there were significant similarities between template and reports based on "look and feel" of documents. Court thought plaintiffs' argument was similar. Court denied plaintiffs' copyright allegations with respect to Quote Builder where plaintiffs' complaint devoid of factual allegations about defendants' alleged access or how they copied or otherwise used Quote Builder.

In Lux Rsch. v. Hull McGuire PC, No. 23-523, 2023 U.S. Dist. LEXIS 166700 (D.D.C. Sept. 19, 2023)

District court dismissed plaintiffs' direct infringement claim against moving defendants—individuals and law firms who represented Proud Boys during 2022 *Nordean* insurrection trial—where plaintiffs' claim was directed at defendants who did not file or join filings containing copyrighted material. To support motion to transfer venue out of Washington, D.C. during Proud Boys trial in 2022, plaintiffs—jury polling company and owner—were hired to conduct study on community attitudes toward January 6 defendants. Plaintiffs interacted primarily with non-moving defendant Hull, completing study and report at Hull's urging but without receiving any of agreed-on $30,000 fee. Defendant Hull represented backing from moving defendants on multiple occasions and submitted plaintiffs' report as attachment to motion to supplement motion to transfer venue, stating it was submitted on behalf of all five defendants. One set of moving defendants filed motion for plaintiff owner to testify in support of motion to transfer venue. After submitting report, plaintiffs asked defendants about payment and received no response. Plaintiffs filed cease-and-desist letter, demanding defendants take down and cease all uses of report. Shortly after, plaintiffs registered report with U.S. Copyright Office and sent additional takedown notice demanding payment based on copyright infringement. Hearing nothing, plaintiffs filed complaint—and later amended complaint—against eight defense lawyers and five law firms involved in *Nordean* case. All defendants other than Hull defendants moved to dismiss plaintiffs' direct copyright infringement claim. Taking moving defendants' lead, court spent majority of discussion on second infringement element—whether defendants infringed plaintiffs' valid copyright. Thrust of plaintiffs' claim was that defendants committed copyright infringement by filing report on *Nordean* public docket. Court agreed with defendants that it was Hull defendants, not moving defendants, who filed report, and plaintiff failed to plausibly plead moving defendants had anything to do with report, let alone reproduced or publicly distributed it. Plaintiff argued moving defendants "joined" three court filings, but two of three filings were before report even existed. Court notes two filings were not "joined" by moving defendants, but were filed by Hull defendants alone, on behalf of Biggs defendant alone, and signed by Hull alone and never joined by moving defendants. Just because Hull defendants stated other defendants joined in extension motion and that report was submitted on behalf of "all five defendants" did not make it so. Only filing that reproduced and distributed report was not joined by moving defendants. Further, moving defendants' alleged inaction in making no attempt to withdraw report from docket could not support direct infringement claim. Plaintiffs had no support for argument that lawyer commits copyright infringement for failing to attempt to remove copyrighted material another lawyer filed or "withdraw" from motion never signed or joined in first place.

Kreatio Software Priv. Ltd. v. IDG Commc'ns, Inc., No. 23-10273, 2024 U.S. Dist. LEXIS 51279 (D. Mass. Mar. 22, 2024)

District court denied defendant internet publishing company's motion to dismiss copyright infringement claim. Plaintiff, software development company, alleged defendant copied elements of software product, which plaintiff licensed to defendant along with another complementary software product. Licensed works were interoperable with each other. During time period in which defendant had access to licensed works, defendant developed own software product, which was similar in nature to primary licensed work and also interoperable with secondary licensed work. As defendant had access to primary licensed work, plaintiff alleged substantial similarity between defendant's work and primary licensed work on bases that defendant's work was interoperable with secondary licensed work and defendant produced defendant's work in faster-than-expected time frame during period in which defendant had access to primary licensed work. Defendant moved to dismiss, arguing plaintiff failed to specifically allege copying by pointing to "exact portions of [primary licensed work] allegedly copied." Court found plaintiff's allegations in complaint adequately pleaded infringement claim, raised "reasonable expectation that discovery will reveal evidence" of infringement, provided "fair notice" to defendant, and asserted "plausible theories to prove substantive similarity." Court thus denied defendant's motion to dismiss infringement claim.

Niehuss v. Colossal Biosciences, Inc., No. 20-617, 2023 U.S.Dist. LEXIS 210071 (W.D. Tex. Nov. 27, 2023)

Magistrate judge recommended that district court deny defendant's motion to dismiss infringement claim, but grant motion to dismiss DMCA claim. Plaintiff, expert in animal illustration, created and registered illustration of extinct dodo bird. Defendant, biotech and genetic engineering company focused on resurrecting extinct species, allegedly used plaintiff's image of dodo for its fundraising. Plaintiff sued for copyright infringement. Defendant moved for dismissal on ground that plaintiff did not identify registration number or append certificate to complaint. Magistrate judge explained that complaint was "short and plain statement of claim," and it was sufficient to allege that plaintiff owned copyright registration even if it was not attached.

Am. Airlines, Inc. v. Spada, No. 23-21844, 2024 U.S. Dist. LEXIS 32525 (S.D. Fla. Feb. 23, 2024)

Court dismissed plaintiff's claim of copyright infringement without prejudice to plaintiff to replead count to apply to individual defendant only and to specify facts supporting cause of action. Plaintiff American Airlines filed complaint followed by first, second, and third amended complaints against various individual defendants. Third amended complaint ("TAC") was filed only against individual

Anthony R. Spada II, alleging, *inter alia*, copyright infringement. Plaintiff claimed Spada was primary coordinator of money laundering scheme involving transfer of money between bank accounts, PayPal accounts, GoFundMe-type accounts, etc. As part of alleged scheme, defendant sent fraudulent emails about job opportunities, whereby defendant and others would pretend to represent someone from American Airlines. In Count V of TAC, plaintiff alleged it had copyright registration for American Airlines Flight Symbol. In addition, it alleged defendant copied its copyrighted images and displayed them in emails sent by Spada and others. Court found that American had pleaded all required elements to state claim for copyright infringement in General Allegations section of TAC. However, it must identify facts it relied on in support of this claim in Count V. Court therefore dismissed Count V without prejudice to American to replead Count to apply to Spada as only defendant and to specify facts supporting cause of action, either by stating them in Count or specifically referring to particular allegations otherwise set forth in pleading.

Trendtex Fabrics, Ltd. v. Bonnie Brown Designs, Inc., No. 23-20291, 2023 U.S. Dist. LEXIS 126598 (S.D. Fla. July 21, 2023)

District court granted in part and denied in part defendant's motion to dismiss complaint. Plaintiffs alleged defendant Bonnie Brown reproduced and sold four items of clothing that infringed copyrighted Hawaiian print surface designs owned by plaintiffs. Bonnie Brown moved to dismiss complaint, alleging under Rule 12(b)(6) that plaintiffs failed to state plausible copyright claim. District court evaluated sufficiency of infringement allegations within complaint. Plaintiffs sufficiently alleged access to protected designs because designs at issue were available, *inter alia*, on two websites and at Trendtex Fabric's place of business. District court also held that complaint set forth sufficient allegations regarding specific, original works that were allegedly copied, and had properly identified its copyright registrations. District court further held that plaintiff had sufficiently alleged that garment at issue was identical or substantially similar to plaintiff's design. Though court observed that at least some of defendant's designs were indistinguishable from plaintiff's, court concluded that such questions should be left for trier of fact. Finally, district court rejected defendant's argument that plaintiff failed to allege whether it was claiming infringement pursuant to direct or secondary liability theory. District court held that language of complaint made clear that plaintiff was alleging direct infringement; plaintiff was not required to use exact phrase "direct infringement" in complaint. District court therefore concluded that plaintiff Trendtex Holding had properly stated plausible claim for direct copyright infringement.

Tomelleri v. SunFrog, LLC, No. 23-10370, 2024 U.S. Dist. LEXIS 38378 (E.D. Mich. Mar. 5, 2024)

District court overruled plaintiff's objections to magistrate's recommendation that plaintiff's complaint be dismissed for failing to plead copyright infringement.

Plaintiff, fresh water fish illustrator, sued defendant, print-on-demand online service provider, for displaying and selling plaintiff's copyright illustrations on defendant's website. Defendant countered that its content was provided by users. Magistrate recommended dismissal of complaint based on plaintiff's failure to allege volitional conduct because defendant's mere display of copyrighted works does not plausibly suggest that defendant knew works were copyrighted. Court overruled plaintiff's objection.

> *Baronius Press Ltd.. v. Faithlife Corp.*, No. 22-1635, 2024 U.S. Dist. LEXIS 17194 (W.D. Wash. Jan. 31, 2024)

District court denied defendant's motion to dismiss infringement claims. Plaintiff, publisher, sued defendant, software company, for alleged infringement of works sold on defendant's software. Defendant admitted unlicensed republication of work was infringing act, but argued plaintiff failed to plausibly assert ownership of copyrights, and that DMCA claims failed because no facts alleged to plausibly establish requisite intent element. Plaintiff alleged ownership of Grundriss copyright, Revised Translation, and Lynch Translation Copyright. Court found plaintiff was not copyright holder of Grundriss copyright but instead owned exclusive license to produce and distribute separate translated work based upon original. Court found license agreement clearly distinguished original work from translated work that was subject of granted license, and licensor reserved all rights in work other than those specifically granted. Court determined plaintiff did not allege any facts to establish ownership. Court found that despite mistaken belief regarding scope of exclusive license, plaintiff made sufficient factual allegations of infringement of exclusive license to publish Revised Translation. Court determined at this stage it must accept as true allegations regarding infringing publication of translation, and cannot test credibility of claims. Court found plaintiff plausibly alleged ownership of Lynch Translation Copyright because alleged and included documents showing assignment of copyright and registration. Court held plaintiff alleged sufficient facts to state plausible claim of infringement as to Revised Translation and Lynch Translation because plaintiff made factual assertion that copyright owner was authorized to assign copyright, and therefore met minimal pleading standard. Court determined plaintiff's infringement claims survived motion so court need not address defendant's arguments regarding lack of injury. Court held plaintiff met minimal pleading standard for asserting intentionality element of DMCA claims because of undisputed factual assertions regarding defendant's alleged prior knowledge.

D. Standing

MMAS Rsch., LLC v. Charite, No. 23-55202, 2024 U.S. App. LEXIS 6004 (9th Cir. Mar. 13, 2024)

Plaintiff medical software company was owner of Morisky Widget, medical software program. Defendant was German hospital. Plaintiff alleged that defendant used plaintiff's work without authorization in medical studies. District court dismissed suit, finding plaintiff lacked standing to sue for infringement because it did not own work and did not allege copyright infringement because it failed to allege infringement in U.S. Plaintiff appealed, arguing, in pertinent part, that district court erred in finding plaintiff lacked standing and in not analyzing claim under Act rather than DMCA. As to standing, Ninth Circuit agreed that district court erred: although plaintiff attempted to enter settlement agreement between itself and Dr. Morisky, agreement was never finalized and therefore plaintiff never fully transferred copyright to Dr. Morisky and court found plaintiff did not abandon its right to sue defendant for infringement. However, court found district court did not err in analyzing claim under Act rather than DMCA. Although plaintiff included DMCA in caption of pleading, it averred no facts in support of such claim or otherwise indicate it was pursuing DMCA claim. Ninth Circuit affirmed dismissal.

Trendtex Fabrics, Ltd. v. Bonnie Brown Designs, Inc., No. 23-20291, 2023 U.S. Dist. LEXIS 126598 (S.D. Fla. July 21, 2023)

District court granted in part and denied in part defendant's motion to dismiss complaint. Plaintiffs Trendtex Holding, LLC and Trendtex Fabrics, Ltd. alleged defendant Bonnie Brown reproduced and sold four items of clothing that infringed copyrighted Hawaiian print surface designs owned by plaintiffs. Bonnie Brown moved to dismiss complaint, alleging that only Trendtex Holding had standing to sue for infringement. District court held that only Trendtex Holding had standing to sue Bonnie Brown, because complaint alleged—and plaintiffs admitted—that all copyrights at issue had been assigned previously to Trendtex Holding, including right to sue for past infringement. District court therefore dismissed Trendtex Fabrics from complaint.

Minden Pictures Inc. v. Ammoland, Inc., No. 20-2276, 2023 U.S. Dist. LEXIS 113697 (D.N.J. June 30, 2023)

Court denied plaintiff's motion for summary judgment and granted defendant's cross motion for summary judgment. Plaintiff licensed wildlife and nature photographs. Work at issue was photograph of two bald eagles on branch seen in snowy weather ("Vezo Work"). Defendant operated Ammoland website and published article entitled "Arizona Governor Brewer Proclaims June 20 American Bald Eagle Day," including copy of Vezo Work that had AMMOLAND logo in place of author and agent's watermark. Plaintiff brought suit for infringement and violation of DMCA, although plaintiff later withdrew DMCA count. Parties cross-moved for summary judgment. Defendant moved for summary judgment on ground that plaintiff did not have standing to bring suit because it was neither registrant nor exclusive licensee of registrant. While plaintiff had earlier agency agreement with plaintiff, that agreement expired under its own terms. Later amendment intended to "clarify" that it was parties' intent that agreement continue in force since effective date did not rectify standing issue; amendment was entered into after complaint was filed and therefore plaintiff lacked standing at time complaint was filed, defect that could not later be cured. Court granted defendant's motion for summary judgment.

InfoGroup Inc. v. Office Depot, Inc., No. 23-80358, 2023 U.S. Dist. LEXIS 106276 (S.D. Fla. June 20, 2023)

District court found plaintiff had Article III standing to bring infringement claim where plaintiff alleged defendant used licensed business marketing data outside scope of license agreement in place between parties. Plaintiff licensed databases consisting of "demographic, marketing and other related information" on millions of businesses ("Works") to defendant to "use the [Works] for its own direct marketing and internal research and analytics." Plaintiff alleged infringement occurred when defendant provided Works to defendant's real estate department for purposes of making real estate decisions, such as choosing retail store locations; plaintiff argued that agreement only permitted use of Works by defendant's marketing department and for direct marketing purposes. Defendant argued plaintiff lacked standing because over course of prior litigation in District of Nebraska, plaintiff's pleadings began with only copyright claim and were expanded to include breach of contract claim, indicating plaintiff was still in process of identifying alleged harm from defendant's use of Works. Court found plaintiff had alleged "sufficiently concrete and non-speculative injury" in claim that defendant "used and made and delivered an unauthorized copy" of Works outside scope of agreement, which "resulted in irreparable harm." According to court, plaintiff's standing was not negatively impacted by "fact that Plaintiff, during the course of discovery and repleading, expanded its legal theory … to include a breach of contract claim and continued to search for precision in discovery about the full scope of its legal theories …."

Estate of Worrell v. Thang, Inc., No. 22-11009, 2024 U.S. Dist. LEXIS 11833 (E.D. Mich. Jan. 23, 2024)

District court granted defendant's motion to dismiss infringement claim because plaintiff lacked standing to assert claims against defendants. Plaintiff, Estate of George "Bernie" Worrell, bandmate and collaborator of George Clinton, filed infringement complaint against defendant SoundExchange, nonprofit collective rights management organization, for allegedly failing to pay royalties from musical works. Plaintiff alleged Worrell was co-author and co-owner of works and therefore entitled to equitable division of royalties. Court found alleged injury arose from Clinton and Thang's denial of Worrell's co-ownership/co-authorship rights under Copyright Act, not administrative services provided by SoundExchange in "collect[ing] digital performance royalties from statutory license users and distribut[ing] those royalties to performing artists and copyright owners." Court found alleged injury fairly traceable only to Clinton and Thang, not to SoundExchange, so plaintiff did not have standing to assert claims against SoundExchange. Court held plaintiff could not show entitlement to royalties unless and until court determined plaintiff was co-owner of works. Court found defendant not entitled to attorneys' fees because dismissal of claim based on standing is without prejudice and defendant is not prevailing party.

Barnes v. Jack Porter, Inc., No. 22-4633, 2023 U.S. Dist. LEXIS 171542 (D.S.C. Sep. 26, 2023)

District court dismissed claims post-dating exclusive copyright license agreement. Plaintiff, photographer, entered into two agreements, granting exclusive license to his photographs to two different entities in turn. Earlier, 2012 agreement contained express list of conveyed rights, which did not address derivate works nor contain catchall provision. By contrast, plaintiff's subsequent December 2019 agreement listed conveyed rights but also had catchall provision stating that exclusive licensee had right to "otherwise use" plaintiff's photographs. In 2016, while attending college football game, plaintiff took photograph of then-college football player Lamar Jackson leaping over opposing team defender. In September 2019, defendant installed mannequin modeled on Jackson's leap during game photographed by plaintiff. In 2021, blog post concerning mannequin appeared on defendant's website. Plaintiff sued for copyright infringement, claiming that he was beneficial owner of copyright in photograph because omission of right to prepare derivative works from exclusive licenses reflected intent that this right remain with plaintiff. Court held that plaintiff had standing to pursue claims related to photograph until execution date of December 2019 agreement, but not thereafter, because lack of catchall phrase in 2012 agreement meant plaintiff retained right to prepare derivative works until entering into 2019 agreement.

E. Miscellaneous

Trendtex Fabrics, Ltd. v. Bonnie Brown Designs, Inc., No. 23-20291, 2023 U.S. Dist. LEXIS 126598 (S.D. Fla. July 21, 2023)

District court granted in part and denied in part defendant's motion to dismiss complaint. Plaintiffs Trendtex Holding, LLC and Trendtex Fabrics, Ltd. alleged defendant reproduced and sold four items of clothing that infringed copyrighted Hawaiian print surface designs owned by plaintiffs. Defendant Bonnie Brown moved to dismiss complaint, alleging that only Trendtex Holding had standing to sue for infringement, alleging under Rule 12(b)(7) that plaintiffs failed to join indispensable party Narmada Textile, and alleging under Rule 12(b)(6) and that plaintiffs failed to state plausible copyright claim. Regarding 12(b)(7) argument, district court first held that absence of Bonnie Brown's supplier Narmada Textile would not prevent complete relief, because parties who participate in copyright infringement are jointly and severally liable. In addition, plaintiffs' allegations indicated that Bonnie Brown and Narmada Textile are part of same distribution chain and infringed same copyright; plaintiffs could therefore choose to pursue full relief against either party. Second, district court concluded that Bonnie Brown had failed to show prejudicial effect from absence of Narmada Textile. In addition, possibility of independent litigation against Narmada Textile would not affect Bonnie Brown's ability to comply with court orders in this case, contrary to Bonnie Brown's assertion. District court accordingly denied Rule 12(b)(7) portion of defendant's motion to dismiss.

II. COPYRIGHTABILITY

A. Originality

Hanagami v. Epic Games, Inc., 85 F.4th 931 (9th Cir. 2023)

Ninth Circuit held that plaintiff had plausibly alleged that his choreography substantially similar to defendant's in-game animations, and reversed district court's grant of motion to dismiss. Plaintiff, choreographer, published YouTube video containing five-minute dance that amassed tens of millions of views. Defendant, videogame company, was creator and developer of Fornite, one of most popular videogames ever, containing extensive virtual world wherein players can purchase "emotes," which are virtual animations performed by avatars in-game. Plaintiff sued, alleging that one of defendant's emotes had copied most recognizable portions of plaintiff's choreography. District court granted defendant's motion to dismiss, holding that plaintiff's choreography was composed of individual poses not protectable when viewed in isolation and that overall steps copied by defendant were not protectable because two-second combination of eight bodily movements was only small component of plaintiff's work. Ninth Circuit reversed, holding that district court erred in applying extrinsic part of substantial similarity test because it reduced plaintiff's choreography to its individual poses, rather than properly comparing selection and arrangement of works' respective elements, including "body position, body shape, body actions, transitions, use of space, timing, pauses, energy, canon, motif, contrast, and repetition." Because district court failed to assess discrete combination of elements of plaintiff's choreography, it erred in holding works not substantially similar at pleading stage. Further, district court erred by holding that plaintiff's choreography was unprotectable merely because it was relatively brief, as plaintiff had more than plausibly alleged that relevant portion had substantial qualitative significance to overall choreography. Ninth Circuit reversed and remanded to district court for further proceedings.

UIRC-GSA Holdings, LLC v. William Blair & Co., LLC, 90 F.4th 908 (7th Cir. 2024)

Court of Appeals held district court did not err in granting appellee's motion for summary judgment because appellant did not have valid copyright in bond documents, since appellant did not create most of language used in documents and language created by appellant was either facts, fragmented phrases, or language dictated by functional considerations. Appellant UIRC-GSA Holdings acquired and managed properties occupied by U.S. government, and developed strategy to offer bonds to market as part of process. To facilitate offering, UIRC produced documents, one of which was created using "Idaho" model sent to UIRC by its lawyers. UIRC later submitted documents to Copyright Office and claimed it only wanted to copyright "additional and revised text" in documents, not "standard legal language." Appellee Blair was financial services company that helped UIRC with bond offering. At same time, third company undertook similar offering. Both UIRC and third company used certain documents during offering process. UIRC showed Blair its copyrighted documents. When UIRC learned Blair was involved in other offering, UIRC sued Blair for copyright infringement. UIRC claimed third party's bond documents were strikingly similar to UIRC's (so much so that they contained references to UIRC). District court granted Blair's motion for summary judgment, deciding UIRC's offering documents could not be subject to copyright protection. Court of Appeals agreed with district court that UIRC's documents were "incredibly similar" to Idaho documents and that non-trivial language UIRC added—facts, short phrases, and functional language—could not be copyrighted. Court noted that UIRC did not independently create most of language in documents at issue. Instead, it copied much of language from Idaho materials and lacked creative expression required for copyright protection. Court highlighted three examples of minimal differences and additions to Idaho sample. Considering UIRC's original language, Court held it was still uncopyrightable because it was only mixture of "fragmented phrases, facts, and language dictated solely by functional considerations." Uncopied portions of bond documents were not creative enough to warrant protection, so court affirmed grant of summary judgment.

Premier Dealer Servs., Inc. v. Allegiance Adm'rs, LLC, 93 F.4th 985 (6th Cir. 2024)

Sixth Circuit affirmed grant of summary judgment for plaintiff, finding that plaintiff's loyalty program certificate was copyrightable and was infringed. Plaintiff managed car dealers' loyalty programs and used loyalty certificates on which terms and conditions of programs appeared. Plaintiff obtained copyright registration for two-page loyalty certificate. Rival company obtained account of former client of plaintiff's and incorporated plaintiff's loyalty certificates into its own loyalty plan, substituting its own contact information and some terms, while preserving certificate's form and appearance, including header and title. District court granted summary judgment for plaintiff, finding that certificate's "dull" subject matter did not preclude it from being original or obtaining copyright protection. Sixth Circuit agreed, finding certificates to contain more than minimal creative spark due to creative choices made in crafting them. Merger did not prevent copyrightability, as record showed that other companies used different ways to express similar idea. Defendant's *scènes à faire* defense failed due to its failure to produce evidence that others in industry expect forms to look like plaintiff's certificate. As certificate was copyrightable and defendant engaged in actual copying, judgment was granted for plaintiff on infringement claim.

Ragan v. Berkshire Hathaway Auto., Inc., 91 F.4th 1267 (8th Cir. 2024)

Eighth Circuit affirmed judgment on pleadings of non-infringement based on non-copyrightability of work. Plaintiff, creator of document titled "Guest Sheet," featuring series of "questions, prompts, headings, fill-in-the-blank lines, and checkboxes" intended for use by car dealerships in selling cars, registered Guest Sheet with Copyright Office. Plaintiff sued car dealership using Guest Sheet for infringement. Defendant successfully moved for judgment on pleadings on basis work not copyrightable, and plaintiff appealed. Eighth Circuit analyzed Guest Sheet, and found that was "basic customer intake sheet containing fewer than 100 words seeking basic information." Reviewing *Feist* and other cases concerning forms "that convey no information," Eighth Circuit found work not entitled to copyright protection. Judgement of non-infringement based on non-copyrightability of work affirmed.

Hines v. BMG Rights Mgmt. (US) LLC, No. 20-3535, 2023 U.S. Dist. LEXIS 170372 (S.D.N.Y. Sept. 25, 2023)

District court granted defendants' motions for summary judgment. Plaintiff Ernie Hines sued defendants W Chappell Music Corporation, and artists Jay-Z, Timbaland, and Ginuwine for alleged use of three-bar guitar riff ("Introduction") at beginning of plaintiff's 1960s composition "Help Me Put Out The Flame (In My Heart)" in defendants' hip-hop songs "Paper Chase" and "Toe 2 Toe." District court agreed with defendants that Introduction was ineligible for copyright protection. Plaintiff's Introduction was drawn from musical device found in 1914 work "Mysterioso Pizzicato" that is in public domain. Defendants' expert noted that at least 28 songs use similar device, and that only distinctions within plaintiff's Introduction were one additional C note, which did not appear in defendants' works, and single note played off beat. District court concluded that addition of single note and single different rhythm was ineligible for protection. Though plaintiff's expert argued that certain other elements in

Introduction were original—for example, picking techniques used to play guitar and selection of particular guitar used to record Introduction—district court declined to consider due to untimely filing of expert's arguments. Further, district court concluded that even if it considered plaintiff's expert's full arguments, it would have reached same decision.

JBrick, LLC v. Chazak Kinder, Inc., No. 21-2883, 2023 U.S. Dist. LEXIS 168647 (E.D.N.Y. Sept. 21, 2023)

District court granted summary judgment for plaintiff dismissing defendant's counterclaim for copyright invalidity. Plaintiff sold LEGO brick sets of its own design of Second Holy Temple based on analysis of Jewish religious texts, and owned copyrights in product itself and in photograph of product. Defendants produced near-replica of product, and plaintiff brought infringement claim. Defendants counterclaimed for copyright invalidity on basis that Second Holy Temple is in public domain, and product thus failed to exhibit sufficient creativity or originality to be entitled to copyright protection. Plaintiff argued that no one knows what Second Holy Temple actually looked like. Court agreed, finding that plaintiff's study of public domain texts in process of designing set was not evidence that product showed no originality. Court found that no reasonable juror could disagree that plaintiff's development of 3D sculpture based on written Jewish religious texts was sufficiently creative to warrant copyright protection.

Thumbtack, Inc. v. Liaison, Inc., No. 23-2830, 2024 U.S. Dist. LEXIS 11022 (N.D. Cal. Jan. 22, 2024)

District court dismissed plaintiff's copyright claim as to text and help pages, but not as to policies. Plaintiff, website owner, sued defendant, operator of competing websites, for infringement for allegedly copying content of plaintiff's website. Court found question whether content of non-discrimination policy, "Review the Pro" policy, privacy policy, policy regarding information collected, and policy regarding updating/deleting and correcting information constituted original, protectible content could not be resolved at motion to dismiss stage, as it must be assessed based on evidence. Court determined use of term "Smart Hiring" could not itself be protected, and placement over stock photo was not protectable as matter of law. Court found plaintiff only alleged copying of titles of Help Pages, but titles not protectible under Compendium. Court gave plaintiff leave to amend to identify with more specificity whether it claimed copyright protection over text of website in entirety.

Simpson Strong-Tie Co. v. MiTek Inc., No. 20-6957, 2023 U.S. Dist. LEXIS 223876 (N.D. Cal. Dec. 15, 2023)

District court held that defendant's copying was *de minimis*. Plaintiff and defendant both designed, manufactured and sold construction products, and each published product catalogs. At issue were abbreviated part names (APIs) used in plaintiff's 2017-2018 and 2019-2020 copyrighted catalogs, each of which contained 20 or fewer new APIs, alphabetically listed alongside previously-included part names. Defendant copied APIs found in both catalogs and plaintiff sued for copyright infringement. Court held that plaintiff's rights extended only to new APIs and not material in earlier versions of catalogs. Although court found most APIs to contain minimal degree of creativity required for copyright protection, defendant's copying when viewed in comparison to entire catalogs was *de minimis* in terms of both quantity (12 APIs in list of 400) and quality (because APIs not source-identifying and indices in which they are located are essentially functional).

Thaler v. Perlmutter, No. 22-1564, 2023 U.S. Dist. LEXIS 145823 (D.D.C. Aug. 18, 2023)

District court granted motion for summary judgment filed by defendant Register of Copyrights, affirming Register's refusal to register visual artwork generated by plaintiff's AI computer system, "Creativity Machine," on basis that work failed to meet human authorship requirement for copyright registration. Sole issue was "whether a work generated entirely by an artificial system absent human involvement should be eligible for copyright"; court agreed with defendants that "human authorship is an essential part of a valid copyright claim." Plaintiff's copyright application stated that work was "autonomously created by a computer algorithm running on a machine," and claimed copyright ownership "as a work-for-hire to the owner of" machine. Court stated that while "copyright law has proven malleable enough to cover works created with or involving technologies developed long after traditional media of writing memorialized on paper," human authorship requirement is established by plain text of Copyright Act and judicial and legislative history of interpretation of copyright law. Plaintiff was unable to point to case in which "a court has recognized copyright in a work originating with a non-human." Plaintiff argued Creativity Machine was "entirely controlled" by him and "the AI only operates at [his] direction," but court found administrative record at Copyright Office included no such claim, so court must operate on presumption work created absent any human involvement. Court held Register properly denied registration due to absence of human authorship.

Fomo Factory, LLC v. Gallery Model Homes, Inc., No. 21-1022, 2023 U.S. Dist. LEXIS 130703 (S.D. Tex. July 28, 2023)

District court denied defendant's motion for summary judgment. Plaintiff alleged infringement of its "immersive art pop-ups," which provided visitors with opportunity to take photographs of themselves or others with creative backdrops and props. Kara Whitten was artist who assisted in creating works for plaintiff, and assigned her works and copyright to plaintiff. Furniture store defendant hired various artists, including Ms. Whitten, to design and install backdrop displays for its in-store furniture. Plaintiff alleged infringement of five copyrighted works. In summary judgment motion, defendant argued that plaintiff's works lacked originality and were not independently created, because elements of works were based on online tutorials, or because they contained *scènes à faire*. However, defendant failed to identify online tutorials allegedly used to create defendant's furniture displays. Though plaintiff's works contained common elements of pinwheels, seesaws, cupcakes, and fringes, district court noted that originality can exist in "unique" expressions of common elements from public domain. In addition, Copyright Office could have declined to register plaintiff's works as whole but did not. Because defendant failed to cite to specific works that existed in public domain prior to plaintiff's works, or other evidence in support of lack of originality, district court concluded that defendant failed to overcome presumption that plaintiff's works were original, and failed to establish as matter of law that plaintiff's works lacked originality.

> *Desirous Parties Unlimited Inc. v. Right Conn. Inc.*, No. 21-1838, 2024 U.S. Dist. LEXIS 40058 (D. Nev. Mar. 6, 2024)

District court denied defendants' motion to dismiss copyright infringement claim because defendants did not properly rebut presumption of originality based on registration, and defendants did not meet summary judgment burden as to actual damages or defendants' profits, or statutory damages or attorneys' fees. Plaintiff alleged defendants copied copyrighted photographs and content on defendants' website. Plaintiff received copyright registration certificates for photographs and content. Court found defendants provided no legal citation or explanation as to why photographs and content unoriginal. Court determined defendants only offered general principals about plaintiff's burden to prove actual damages or defendants' profits from alleged copyright infringement, and defendants did not explain plaintiff's lack of evidence or providing any citations to record. Court found dispute over material fact existed regarding whether defendants commenced new use of plaintiff's copyrighted materials after effective date of copyright registrations.

B. Compilations and Derivative Works

> *Widespread Elec. Sales, LLC v. Upstate Breaker Wholesale Supply, Inc.*, No. 20-2541, 2023 U.S. Dist. LEXIS 224054 (N.D. Tex. Dec. 17, 2023)

Court found plaintiff owned valid copyrights in four registered works, but that only portions of plaintiff's works were protectible. Founder of plaintiff company, seller of obscure and obsolete electrical products, created website in 2008. Founder chose products, arranged product pages with information (part number, product description and specifications, and photos), and spent "countless hours" typing product pages and creating database. To protect website and database, plaintiff applied for and received four Group Registrations for automated databases. Defendant company, also seller of electrical equipment, was founded in 2013. Defendant used scraping tool to copy text from plaintiff's website despite several anti-scraping and anti-spidering warnings on plaintiff's site. In 2020, plaintiff realized defendant had copied hundreds of thousands of plaintiff's product pages. Plaintiff sued for copyright infringement. Following close of discovery, both parties brought partial summary judgment motions. Court considered them together. Court first found plaintiff to be owner of both derivative works (product pages) and preexisting works (database). Court then evaluated what elements of plaintiff's work were protected by copyright. Court agreed with defendant that product information itself was not copyrightable because it was merely facts. Product descriptions listed product's factual specifications, including functional and technical data, with no original written expression. While product information was public domain, court found that plaintiff's selection and arrangement of facts comprising product descriptions had minimal degree of creativity and therefore were entitled to copyright protection as compilations. Court made same finding for plaintiff's selection and arrangement of product accessories, similar products, and product specifications on website. Part numbers were not eligible for copyright protection because they lacked creative expression. Court also found plaintiff's selection and arrangement of product offerings in its product pages and aggregate of those pages compromising database were protected by its valid copyrights.

C. Pictorial, Graphic and Sculptural Works

AFG Media Ltd. v. Poptrend-Official, No. 23-1840, 2023 U.S. Dist. LEXIS 230686 (W.D. Pa. Dec. 29, 2023)

Plaintiff seller of costumes owned copyright in design of alien costume with features that "give[] the viewer the impression that a person is being carried around by an alien." Plaintiff sued group of e-commerce sellers alleging infringement by selling knock-off alien costumes. After court issued temporary restraining order, plaintiff moved for preliminary injunction. Arguing against preliminary injunction, defendants asserted that plaintiff's copyright in costume was invalid because costume was "useful article" and not sculpture. Copyrightable aspect of costume was not that "sculptural features in combination depict a large alien holding up a man," but rather that combination of color, shape, and size of alien in conjunction with combination of color, shape, and size of man being held would be subject to copyright protection. District court rejected defendants' argument that copyright was invalid because costume lacked originality, finding evidence proffered by defendants of other alien costumes on market insufficient to show that costume lacked originality. Defendants' copyright invalidity argument rejected, and court maintained presumption that plaintiff had valid copyright in work.

D. Miscellaneous

Enos v. Walt Disney Co., No. 23-5790, 2024 U.S. Dist. LEXIS 39705 (C.D. Cal. Mar. 4, 2024)

District court denied defendants' motion to dismiss because plaintiff's character was copyrightable. Plaintiffs created Honu, Hawaiian sea turtle with blue eyes who plays ukulele, as part of songs, books, live theatrical performances, and other products. Defendants, collectively Disney, unveiled group of characters at Hawaiian resort that included Olu Mel, turtle with blue eyes who plays ukulele. Plaintiffs alleged that Disney illegally copied Honu in creating Olu and Disney moved to dismiss, arguing that Honu insufficiently delineated and distinct to merit copyright protection. Court held that, though "precise nature" of Honu's appearance changed across iterations, plaintiffs had alleged that Honu was sufficiently delineated because he was consistently presented as bright green-and-yellow Hawaiian sea turtle with blue eyes, long eyelashes, nostrils and spots on his flippers, along with musical traits (such as carrying ukulele). Moreover, plaintiffs had sufficiently pled distinctiveness because it was plausible that Honu's irises and facial structure were plaintiffs' original expression (rather than being derived from natural turtle stock elements) and Honu's musicality was character trait that did not derive from ideas of turtles in their natural surroundings.

Laatz v. Zazzle, Inc., No. 22-4844, 2024 U.S. Dist. LEXIS 4838 (N.D. Cal. Jan. 9, 2024)

District court denied plaintiff's motion for summary judgment on copyright claim related to defendants' distribution of fonts she created for license. Plaintiff alleged that defendants, operators of online design platform Zazzle, fraudulently obtained license to use software containing three fonts created by plaintiff, and violated license by making fonts available to millions of people on Zazzle platform, including for commercial use. On plaintiff's copyright infringement claim, parties disputed whether plaintiff's copyrights in fonts were valid. Plaintiff obtained registrations for fonts five years and two days after date of first publication, just missing five-year deadline for registrations to be prima facie evidence of validity. Court also found that even if registrations had been timely, defendants presented substantial evidence to potentially overcome presumption of validity, including that plaintiff created fonts on existing software, and not original software. Parties also had rival experts on copyrightability of fonts. Court found sufficient disputes of fact to deny summary judgment.

SnagPod, LLC v. Precision Kiosk Techs., Inc., No. 23-10401, 2023 U.S. Dist. LEXIS 183732 (E.D. Mich. Oct. 12, 2023)

District court granted defendant's motion for judgment on pleadings. Plaintiff sued defendant, alleging infringement of various breathalyzer, alcohol testing, and kiosk technologies. Plaintiff claimed copyright in "sequence, structure, organization, and user interface of the input and output forms" of works. Defendant argued in response that shared elements between parties' respective software products were "necessary 'components of, or steps in, a computer alcoholic breathalyzer system … unprotectable under the doctrines of merger and *scènes à faire*…" Court agreed with defendant, noting that plaintiff had not alleged copying of any specific source code, and to extent that plaintiff sought protection for any copyrightable expressive components of works, like works' layout, format, and color scheme, defendant had, as factual matter, not copied them. Court noted that shared features of parties' software products, such as welcome page, "Enter Your User ID" page, "Take Your Photo" page, "Creating Fingerprint Records" page, "Fingerprint Authorization" page, "Alcohol Testing" pages, and "Alcohol Test Completed" pages, and their sequence, structure, and organization, were so essential to and embedded in operation of alcohol breathalyzer kiosk as to be precluded from copyright protection under merger and *scènes à faire* doctrines. Court granted defendant's motion for judgment on pleadings, finding defendant had not copied any copyrightable elements of works.

III. OWNERSHIP

A. Works Made for Hire

Softketeers, Inc. v. Regal West Corp., No. 19-519, 2023 U.S. Dist. LEXIS 233249 (C.D. Cal. Dec. 26, 2023)

District court denied defendant's post-jury trial motion for judgment as matter of law that software at issue was work for hire. Plaintiff, software development company, created and maintained several computer software programs used by defendant logistics company. After terminating relationship with defendant, plaintiff sued for, *inter alia*, infringement of copyright in software. Following trial, defendant moved for judgment as matter of law that (contrary to jury's determination) plaintiff and plaintiff's developers were effectively defendant's employees and therefore software programs were works for hire owned by defendant. Court found that ample evidence supported jury's finding that programs were written by independent contractors, including that: plaintiff controlled manner and means of software development; defendant did not provide equipment to, or control schedules of, software developers; bulk of work performed at, and source code stored in servers in, plaintiff's offices; and defendant's main business was logistics rather than software.

B. Transfer of Ownership

Patrick v. Poree, No. 23-12732, 2023 U.S. App. LEXIS 33078 (11th Cir. Dec. 14, 2023)

Eleventh Circuit affirmed denial of default judgment on infringement claim, finding plaintiff failed to establish copyright ownership. Plaintiff, former manager of musical artist BOZZ Lay'dee, sued artist for infringement of copyright in song titled "I Do What I Want," alleging that plaintiff was "exclusive owner" of sound recording and that artist's performance of song (which was featured on episode of Lizzo's television show "Watch Out for the Big Grrrls") constituted infringement. Defendant failed to respond to or defend claims, and plaintiff filed motion for default judgment. District court denied motion for default judgment, finding plaintiff did not have valid copyright claim because she failed to establish ownership of valid copyright in work; plaintiff appealed denial of default judgment to Eleventh Circuit. Eleventh Circuit found plaintiff failed to acquire ownership of copyright, as she was not author or co-author of work, nor was there valid transfer of ownership. Eleventh Circuit rejected plaintiff's argument that listing of her name under "Rights and Permissions" on copyright registration conferred ownership, noting that such listing only "made her the person to contact for permission to use" work. Eleventh Circuit similarly rejected plaintiff's assertion that she received ownership via "verbal agreement" with co-authors of work, noting that plaintiff never identified "statutorily required written transfer" of copyright ownership. Finding that plaintiff failed to establish claim, Eleventh Circuit affirmed denial of motion for default judgment.

C. Termination of Transfers

Merrill v. Hyman, No. 22-2971, 2024 U.S. App. LEXIS 1140 (2d Cir. Jan. 18, 2024)

Second circuit affirmed district court ruling that plaintiff could not terminate agreement because agreement was royalties agreement that cannot be terminated. Plaintiff sued defendant seeking declaratory judgment that she could terminate, pursuant to § 304(c), agreement between plaintiff's late husband and defendant, which granted defendant certain rights related to plaintiff's husband's lyrics for Broadway musical *Funny Girl.* Plaintiff argued she could revoke agreement under termination-of-transfers provision of Copyright Act. Court found plain language of agreement showed plaintiff's late husband was not selling or licensing to defendant any of his rights under Act, but rather rights to financial compensation he had received and would receive by virtue of copyright rights in lyrics. Court found agreement never defined copyright right being transferred or specified nature of any license to use lyrics. Court held agreement did not transfer or license copyright or rights under copyright in lyrics; district court thus correctly determined that this was royalties agreement that sold financial rights, and that plaintiff cannot terminate such agreement under Copyright Act.

Moss v. Miller, No. 23-7424, 2023 U.S. Dist. LEXIS 226013 (C.D. Cal. Dec. 15, 2023)

District court dismissed declaratory relief claim brought by two of decedent's children. Songwriter Ron Miller died in 2007. At that time his estranged wife Aurora Miller became entitled to 50% interest, and each of Ron's four children became entitled to 12.5% interest, in Ron's termination interests with respect to copyrights in songs he had written. Complaint alleged that one child, Lisa, improperly influenced Aurora for purpose of using their combined majority interest in copyright termination interests to execute numerous notices of termination from August 2009 through April 2016, with several allegedly executed after Aurora lacked capacity to understand, consent to, or execute legal documents, and two allegedly executed after Aurora was in coma and "essentially brain dead." In 2018 Lisa's half-siblings warned plaintiffs "that Lisa was up to something regarding Ron's song catalogue, which prompted [Plaintiffs] to investigate." In early 2019, plaintiffs discovered existence of allegedly invalid termination notices via Copyright Office's records." In March 2019, plaintiffs notified Sony that termination notices were invalid, unenforceable, and ineffective. Lisa eventually signed publishing deal with Sony and began releasing her own re-recordings of Ron's songs in April 2019. Plaintiffs sought declaration that 38 termination notices were invalid, ineffective, and unenforceable because Lisa did not have right to exercise them on behalf of Aurora and because notices failed to comply with statutory requirements under Copyright Act. Court noted that three-year statute of limitations found in § 507(b) apples to copyright ownership claims, which accrue "when plain and express repudiation" of ownership is communicated to claimant, and are barred three years from time of repudiation. Claims tied to termination-notice issues are treated as ownership claims, and are thus subject to that repudiation-based focus. Complaint itself revealed that, before September 7, 2020 (i.e., three years before plaintiffs filed complaint), plaintiffs had: (1) been warned by Lisa's half-siblings that Lisa was "up to something," which caused plaintiffs to investigate; (2) discovered existence of notices via Copyright Office's records; (3) notified Sony that termination notices were invalid, unenforceable, and ineffective; and (4) after months of attempting to reach resolution with Lisa, been met with behavior from Lisa where she "became obstinate, refusing to answer basic questions or provide documents about the Invalid Termination Notices, including the alleged basis for Lisa's authority to send the Invalid Termination Notices on behalf of Aurora." Plaintiffs argued that law required any repudiation to have been communicated to them *by* Lisa, not simply that plaintiffs acquired information that led to potential ownership dispute. Court disagreed; under Ninth Circuit law "claims of co-ownership ... accrue when plain and express repudiation of co-ownership is communicated to the claimant, and are barred three years from the time of repudiation." Plaintiffs could have taken action, but did not do so—possibly, court noted, because plaintiffs may have hoped an out-of-court resolution could have been obtained. But "possession of a hope does not excuse inaction." Court accordingly dismissed plaintiffs' declaratory relief claim with prejudice.

> *Livingston v. Jay Livingston Music, Inc.*, No. 22-532, 2024 U.S. Dist. LEXIS 29398 (M.D. Tenn. Feb. 21, 2024)

District court dismissed declaratory judgment complaint because plaintiff failed to allege any deficiencies in termination notices and alternately requested relief was not justiciable. Jay Livingston was composer of many famous songs, including "Que Sera, Sera" ("Whatever Will Be, Will Be"). Defendant—Livingstone's daughter Travilyn—served two termination notices under § 203 seeking to terminate grant of rights relating to "Que Sera, Sera" and several other compositions. Plaintiff—Travilyn's own daughter, Tammy—brought suit seeking declaration that termination notices were ineffective or, alternately, that they do not affect her right to receive royalties from compositions. Court granted defendant's motion to dismiss because plaintiff's arguments that Tammy lacked authority to terminate grants either expressly contradicted documents provided by Tammy (including documents related to issues already ruled upon by probate court) or were entirely unmoored from relevant law (because § 203 does not limit termination rights to entity to which author initially granted his rights). Moreover, because notices complied with § 203's requirements, there was no substantive reason to disregard them. Tammy's alternative request for declaration that she was still entitled to royalties from outside United States was not justiciable because it was conceded by defendant.

D. Joint Works and Co-Ownership

> *Gentile v. Doyle*, No. 21-8528, 2024 U.S. Dist. LEXIS 1369 (S.D.N.Y. Jan. 2, 2024)

District court dismissed plaintiffs' claims where their contributions to script insufficient to render them sole or co-authors. Plaintiffs claimed they had collaborated with former defendant on first portion of script about madam running brothel in 1860s Wyoming ("First Script"), which former defendant registered as sole author. Plaintiffs then worked with defendant Doyle on additional script ("Second Script"), alleging that they were sole authors but that Doyle had contributed to script, characters, setting, stage direction and dialogue of Second Script, albeit at plaintiffs' explicit direction. Doyle registered Second Script, and Plaintiffs subsequently registered Second Script themselves. After claims against former defendant were dismissed, plaintiffs amended complaint to seek declaration that they were sole authors of Second Script. Court granted Doyle's motion to dismiss because plaintiffs' own allegations established that Doyle was at least coauthor of Second Script. Plaintiffs' claims that Doyle's contributions made at their explicit direction were irrelevant because elements plaintiffs claimed to have "authored" or "dictated" were broad, uncopyrightable ideas that were not translated into any tangible mediums of expression that would support sole authorship claim.

> *That One Video Ent. LLC v. Koil Content Creation Pty Ltd.*, No. 23-2687, 2024 U.S. Dist. LEXIS 27005 (C.D. Cal. Feb. 14, 2024)

District court denied defendants' motion to dismiss because plaintiff was not required to obtain copyright registration before seeking declaratory judgment of joint ownership. Plaintiff, content creator company employing individuals in videogame industry, employed software developer, Daniel Tracey, whose services plaintiff was permitted to sell to third parties. Defendants, operators of videogame server, contracted to obtain Tracey's services as independent contractor in exchange for 50% of game revenue, without executing agreement that Tracey's contributions were works for hire. After Tracey was terminated due to personal dispute, plaintiff sent letter to defendants asserting exclusive ownership over Tracey's contributions to defendants' server and noting that it had significant copyright infringement claims against defendants. Plaintiff then sought declaration that it was joint owner of Tracey's contributions, which defendants moved to dismiss on ground it was disguised copyright infringement claim that could not be pursued until plaintiff obtained copyright registration. Court denied defendants' motion, noting that plaintiff properly asserted joint ownership claim, which was essential to determining whether it was entitled to accounting of profits from defendants. Plaintiff's earlier assertion of infringement claims in demand letter was irrelevant to determining claims actually asserted in action.

> *Softketeers, Inc. v. Regal West Corp.*, No. 19-519, 2023 U.S. Dist. LEXIS 233249 (C.D. Cal. Dec. 26, 2023)

District court denied defendant's post-jury trial motion for judgment as matter of law that software at issue was jointly authored. Plaintiff, software development company, created and maintained several computer software programs used by defendant logistics company. After terminating relationship with defendant, plaintiff sued for, *inter alia*, infringement of copyright in software. Following trial, defendant moved for judgment as matter of law that (contrary to jury's determination) at least two of defendant's employees co-authored software code. Court declined to disturb jury's verdict because defendant's employees contributed less than 160 out of tens of thousands of lines of code and there was testimony that plaintiff did not use even that code.

Halperin v. Goodman, No. 20-7616, 2024 U.S. Dist. LEXIS 16026 (N.D. Ill. Jan. 30, 2024)

District court granted plaintiff's request for declaratory judgment, holding that plaintiff was sole copyright holder in educational video lessons that she created. Plaintiff, creator of lessons designed to improve children's handwriting and fine motor skills, entered into joint venture with defendants to make her video lessons accessible via online platform. Defendants provided funding for website and made minor, non-substantive edits to videos (such as adding intros/outros and requesting removal of background noise). When joint venture ran out of money, defendants sought funding from third party, which predicated investment on plaintiff's assignment of her intellectual property rights in videos to third parties. Plaintiff refused and proposed licensing agreement, which was never signed. Defendants subsequently uploaded plaintiff's videos to YouTube without her knowledge or consent. Plaintiff sued for declaration that she was sole holder of copyright in videos. Court held that there was no evidence that parties intended to be joint authors and, indeed, all materials credited only plaintiff as author of videos and one of individual defendants expressly stated that videos not intended to be joint works. Moreover, defendants' only contributions to videos were minor, non-substantive edits that did not rise to level of being copyrightable.

Beard v. Helman, No. 21-680, 2024 U.S. Dist. LEXIS 39622 (M.D. Pa. Mar. 6, 2024)

On summary judgment, district court held that defendant was joint author of one work, but not another. Plaintiff, fantasy artist, presented two-dimensional dragon drawing ("Original Design") to defendant, Renaissance fair leather goods seller, to enable defendant to create, pursuant to oral licensing agreement, dragon-themed boot buttons (and, according to defendant, other goods). In turning Original Design into three-dimensional boot button, defendant rejected up to 20 models, prepared by Mexican contractors, before receiving simplified rendering that was satisfactory and capable of reproduction in metal ("Simplified Design"). Defendant then forged three-dimensional boot buttons based on Simplified Design and also used Simplified Design on other products, mainly through leather appliques. Court held that defendant was joint author of boot buttons because adapting Original Design to new medium rose above *de minimis* contribution where it required exercise of intellectual creativity and discretion, and because there was no dispute that parties intended their contributions to be merged into inseparable unitary whole with regard to boot buttons. However, defendant was not joint author of Simplified Design, which was derivative only of plaintiff's independent Original Design and did not require creativity. Moreover, issues of fact existed as to parties' intent with regard to products other than boot buttons.

E. Contracts and Licenses

Loeb-Defever v. Mako, LLC, No. 22-20362, 2023 U.S. App. LEXIS 23004 (5th Cir. Aug. 30, 2023)

Circuit court affirmed district court's grant of summary judgment to defendants on infringement and DMCA claims. Plaintiff, architect, sued defendants, developers for senior living facility, for infringement and violations of DMCA for allegedly using plaintiff's copyrighted schematics to develop facility. Plaintiffs granted defendants express, nonexclusive license to use preliminary design in connection with project. Parties argued over scope of license. Court found contract granted defendants license to use schematics to create derivative works because gave right to reproduce, and provisions suggested discretion to distribute and use schematics throughout project. Court determined contract title and relevant provisions established parties intended schematics to be used both for financing purposes and as conceptual springboard for later design stages. Court found contract allowed for express authorization of defendant to use third parties to implement license. Court held defendants' use of preliminary design schematics to create derivative works and subsequent marketing, rental, and sale of facilities did not exceed scope of license. Court held plaintiff failed to establish genuine dispute of DMCA claim because defendants could not have intended or known conduct would induce, enable, facilitate, or conceal infringement when they were not infringing copyright because they held license.

Wanjuan Media (Tianjin) Co., Ltd. v. Amazon.Com, Inc., No. 22-1434, 2024 U.S. Dist. LEXIS 41209 (S.D.N.Y. Mar. 8, 2024)

Plaintiff television production and distribution company based in Tianjin, China claimed ownership of Chinese language historical drama television show General and I, and sued Amazon for infringement for streaming work via Amazon Prime. On cross motions for summary judgment, defendant Amazon alleged it held valid license to work, and plaintiff argued license invalid because party to license with Amazon did not hold rights to work. Tracing history of work, district court found that plaintiff entered into TV Series Joint Production agreement concerning work with Chinese media company "Croton Culture"; plaintiff then alleged that it entered into Joint Distribution Agreement transferring rights in work from Croton Culture to "Croton Film and TV" (validity of this agreement disputed by Amazon); Croton Culture entered into distribution agreement with DramaFever for online distribution of work; and Amazon entered into agreement with DramaFever to broadcast its catalog of content via Amazon Prime streaming service. Amazon argued that purported transfer of rights from Croton Culture to Croton Film and TV was invalid, and thus it had valid unbroken licensing chain granting it right to distribute work, thus overcoming any infringement claim. Plaintiff argued transfer was valid, and that Croton Film and TV did not have rights to sublicense work to Amazon. Amazon specifically argued transfer to Croton Film and TV was invalid because language of agreement stated "[t]his Agreement shall become effective when it is duly signed by the authorized signatories of Party A, Party B and Party C, and affixed with the seals of all the Parties," but "Party B" (plaintiff's predecessor) only affixed its seal and did not sign agreement. Analyzing Chinese contract law, district court found agreement "expressly and unambiguously requires the signatures and seals of all three parties for the agreement to be executed," and absent compliance with such requirements agreement is invalid. District court concluded that Amazon had valid license to stream work, and granted defendant's motion for summary judgment on infringement.

Elohim Epf United States, Inc. v. 162 D & y Corp., No. 19-2431, 2023 U.S. Dist. LEXIS 224891 (S.D.N.Y. Dec. 18, 2023)

District court held that foreign copyright management organization's records insufficient to defeat assignment of rights to plaintiff. Non-party songwriter Brave Brother assigned to non-party Elohim Korea exclusive rights to administer certain Korean-language compositions in United States, Canada and Japan. Elohim Korea, pursuant to subpublishing agreement, assigned to plaintiff Elohim USA exclusive rights to administer compositions in United States and Canada. Plaintiff registered compositions, including seven disputed works at issue in case, with U.S. Copyright Office before suing defendants, karaoke establishments, for infringing plaintiff's public performance rights. Defendants urged that records maintained by non-party Korean Music Copyright Association (KOMCA), collective copyright administration non-profit, showed that Brave Brother had assigned worldwide publication rights in disputed works to non-party MelodyGallery (rather than Elohim Korea). According to KOMCA records, MelodyGallery then conditionally transferred copyrights for six of seven disputed works to non-party Enablefind, except excluded United States from transfer. Court held that KOMCA records did not defeat assignment of Brave Brother's U.S. publishing rights to Elohim Korea, and subsequently to plaintiff, because KOMCA did not require registration of agreements for exploitation of works outside Korea (like subpublishing agreement). Moreover, subpublishing agreement expressly covered United States, while transfer from MelodyGallery to Enablefind excluded United States.

Norris v. Goldner, No. 19-5491, 2023 U.S. Dist. LEXIS 151689 (S.D.N.Y. Aug. 24, 2023)

District court granted plaintiff webcomic artist's motion for summary judgment as to infringement claim where defendants, board game publisher and his companies, used plaintiff's preexisting artwork in trademark applications without permission. Plaintiff, artist and creator of "Blob" character and "Webcomic Name" brand, contracted with defendants to make Blob-themed game and plush toy. Contract assigned defendants rights to planned game and toy, but plaintiff retained rights to his existing artwork. Defendants filed trademark applications using plaintiff's work without permission, including Webcomic Name's Facebook page and shop page, plaintiff's Patreon page showing Blob, and several Blob comics. Defendants argued they were authorized by contract to use images; plaintiff disagreed. Court analyzed scope of contract, rejecting defendants' argument that some images were created after parties entered into contract, noting there was no such evidence. In fact, indisputable evidence showed that at least some images defendants used in trademark applications were created before contract, thus forming part of plaintiff's existing brand and artwork. Court analyzed language of contract to reject another of defendants' arguments, that they were contractually immune from plaintiff's claim of infringement as to works post-dating agreement. Court also pointed out defendants' access to plaintiff's online accounts did not transfer ownership over assets therein or give defendants license for their future use. Court ultimately determined contract was limited to planned board game and stuffed animal but did not convey broad rights to plaintiff's existing artwork and characters. Defendants therefore infringed plaintiff's copyright by using plaintiff's preexisting artwork in trademark applications without permission, and plaintiff was entitled to summary judgment on this claim.

Williams v. D'Youville Coll., No. 21-1001, 2024 U.S. Dist. LEXIS 23979 (W.D.N.Y. Feb. 9, 2024)

Plaintiffs, group of former professors at D'Youville College, sued college and associated entities for infringement of joint work bearing title "A Professional Masters Degree in Education: A detailed guide from planning to implementation." Defendants moved to dismiss for failure to state claim. On direct infringement claim, plaintiffs alleged defendants infringed by "sharing … duplicating … and using [the work] to create derivative works, including adapted instructional materials" without permission. In moving to dismiss infringement claim, defendants argued that plaintiffs only alleged infringement via "syllabus," which defendants used pursuant to union contract with plaintiffs, and that plaintiffs failed to allege any portion of works improperly copied outside of license. Plaintiffs argued that although license did grant defendants right to use "syllabus," work at issue was not merely "syllabus," in part because work contained "assignment and guidelines for completing the assignment, content that is outside of the license." Reviewing materials and definition of "syllabus" within license, district court found work contained more information than mere syllabus, including complete text of article authored by one of plaintiffs. Finding portions of copied work outside of license grant, court denied motion to dismiss infringement claim.

Chaquico v. Jefferson Starship, Inc., No. 22-4907, 2024 U.S. Dist. LEXIS 53153 (N.D. Cal. Mar. 25, 2024)

District court granted defendants' motion for summary judgment on counterclaim for deduction of costs and expenses when calculating plaintiff's share of royalties. Plaintiff, musician and songwriter, contributed to defendants' album and sought royalty payments under written termination agreement. Defendants counterclaimed, arguing they were allowed to deduct costs and expenses when calculating plaintiff's share of royalties. Court found plaintiff entitled to publishing royalties for songs he wrote because plaintiff held copyrights in musical compositions. Court found plaintiff entitled to artist royalties for performing on records, but records were works for hire, so royalties did not arise from copyright law. Court determined termination agreement plainly supported interpretation that prohibition against imposing fees, commissions, or other charges related only to publishing royalties, not artist royalties. Court found parties plainly understood band share would continue to be assessed against total artist royalties when calculating plaintiff's share of royalties, so no basis to conclude defendants cannot charge management fees or similar expenses against total artist royalties when calculating plaintiff's share.

Softketeers, Inc. v. Regal West Corp., No. 19-519, 2023 U.S. Dist. LEXIS 233249 (C.D. Cal. Dec. 26, 2023)

District court denied defendant's post-jury trial motion for judgment as matter of law that defendant had implied license to use and modify software. Plaintiff, software development company, created and maintained several computer software programs used by defendant logistics company. After terminating relationship with defendant, plaintiff sued for, *inter alia*, infringement of copyright in software. Following trial, defendant moved for judgment as matter of law that (contrary to jury's determination) defendant had implied license to use and modify plaintiff's software. It was undisputed that parties had ongoing, 18-year relationship and that plaintiff did not use written contracts in its dealings with defendant. In terms of plaintiff's intent, plaintiff testified that it did not provide defendant with source code (which would have allowed defendant to modify or continue using it) while defendant testified that plaintiff's delivery of executable code was functionally equivalent to source code. Although court did not regard evidence in plaintiff's favor as particularly compelling, there was nevertheless room for jury to draw inferences in plaintiff's favor and therefore verdict was not disturbed.

Roskovensky v. Sanibel Captiva Island Vacation Rentals, LLC, No. 22-602, 2024 U.S. Dist. LEXIS 45778 (M.D. Fla. Mar. 15, 2024)

District court denied plaintiff's motion for summary judgment, and granted in part and denied in part defendant's cross-motion for summary judgment. Plaintiff photographer took photos of vacation rental property for defendant property management and marketing company. Plaintiff's photos included photos taken of interior of property and exterior of property before defendant took over management of property. Plaintiff agreed to license certain pre-existing photos to defendant. At request of defendant, plaintiff also later took second set of photos of interior of property. Plaintiff alleged defendant's use of pre-existing photos exceeded scope of license agreement, and therefore constituted infringement, because defendant used pre-existing Interior Photos in promotion of property when license only applied to pre-existing exterior photos. Furthermore, plaintiff alleged defendant's use of pre-existing exterior photos exceeded scope of licensing agreement because defendant used pre-existing exterior photos following end of alleged term of license. Finally, plaintiff alleged defendant used second set of photos without authorization. Defendant argued it held non-exclusive license to use pre-existing interior photos and second set of photos, and pointed to correspondences between plaintiff and defendant in which plaintiff provided photos to defendant. For all pre-existing photos, court granted defendant's motion for summary judgment, finding plaintiff's invoice to defendant for pre-existing photos included license to "images" and term "images" was modified by plaintiff's provision of "image download link," which linked to download page for all pre-existing photos. Accordingly, court found all pre-existing photos were subject to plaintiff's license to defendant. Furthermore, court found invoice enclosing photo download link including contradictory terms regarding duration of license, indicating license would be for both 90 days and six months. Court applied Florida contract law, which requires ambiguity in contract to be construed against drafting party, and found term of license to be six months, so defendant's use of pre-existing photos after 90 days did not exceed scope of license because such use was before end of six-month time period. As such, plaintiff's motion was denied and defendant's motion was granted as to those allegations. Finally, as to infringement allegations regarding second set of photos, court found genuine dispute of material fact as to whether plaintiff provided implied license to defendant, as defendant requested plaintiff to create second set of photos and plaintiff delivered second set of photos via email and said second set of photos was "finished and ready for use"; previous invoice for pre-existing photos said fee would "be applied towards … the new reshoot photo session"; plaintiff previously allowed defendant to use pre-existing photos before payment of license fee; and plaintiff's email correspondence did not warn defendant would be infringing if defendant used second set of photos before paying license fee. Given outstanding questions of material fact relating to potential implied license for second set of photos, court denied defendant's motion for summary judgment as to second set of photos.

Trent P. Fisher Enters., LLC v. SAS Automation, LLC, No. 20-216, 2023 U.S. Dist. LEXIS 135933 (S.D. Ohio Aug. 3, 2023)

District court denied defendants' motion for summary judgment on plaintiffs' claim that defendant breached license agreement. Plaintiffs sold defendant SAS to defendants Piab USA, Inc. and Piab AB. As part of transaction, plaintiffs transferred equity in SAS to Piab, but Piab assigned IP rights in SAS's proprietary e-commerce software ("Works") to plaintiffs to be licensed back to Piab. Works were developed in significant part with code from open-source e-commerce software OpenCart pursuant to GNU General Public License ("GPL"), obliging developers to publicly disclose source code and make work available for free use if software developed via GPL is "covered work" and "conveyed" to third party. When Piab developed in-house e-commerce software largely based on source code from Works, plaintiff sued for infringement, claiming that defendant's use of Works exceeded scope of license agreement. Defendants moved for summary judgment but court denied motion, finding that plaintiffs' claims would fail or succeed depending on extent to which plaintiffs establish Works are covered by GPL, since plaintiffs would have no ability to restrict usage of works covered by GPL in license agreement.

Oliver v. Meow Wolf, Inc., No. 20-237, 2023 U.S. Dist. LEXIS 104919 (D.N.M. June 16, 2023)

District court held that plaintiff granted defendant irrevocable implied license to market her work, but factual issue remained as to whether work could be marketed under different name. In 2016, plaintiff installed visual artwork called Ice Station Quellette ("ISQ") in permanent exhibition called House of Eternal Return ("HER"), receiving $1,000 labor budget from defendant. Plaintiff rejected defendant's request that ISQ be renamed. Defendant marketed HER using images of ISQ and had various (ultimately not fruitful) discussions with plaintiff about potential derivative works of ISQ character. In 2018, plaintiff requested removal of ISQ and, when defendant did not comply, sued. Court had previously granted defendant summary judgment on plaintiff's copyright infringement claims based on display of ISQ in HER, and now so granted on claims based on use of ISQ images to market and promote HER. It was undisputed that plaintiff, in response to request from agent for HER, created ISQ installation within HER with intent that it be publicly displayed at HER. Moreover, plaintiff necessarily intended that defendant use images of ISQ to promote HER because plaintiff believed she would receive share of HER's revenue and defendant's promotion resulted in higher revenues. Plaintiff's belated request that images of ISQ not be used did not weigh on plaintiff's objective intent at time she created and delivered work. However, issue of fact existed as to whether defendant could use images of ISQ under different name.

F. Miscellaneous

Valancourt Books, LLC v. Garland, 82 F.4th 1222 (D.C. Cir. 2023)

D.C. Circuit reversed grant of summary judgment for Copyright Office, finding that Office worked unconstitutional taking when it demanded that copyright holder relinquish physical copies of copyrighted books on pain of fines. Section 407 of Copyright Act requires owner of copyright to deposit two copies of work with Library of Congress. Copyright office enforces this requirement by issuing demand letters that noncomplying owners must either deposit copies or pay fine. Upon receiving such letter, plaintiff protested that it could not afford to deposit copies. Plaintiff sued Register of Copyrights and Attorney General, challenging deposit requirement in Section 407 as unconstitutional taking of property in violation of Fifth Amendment and invalid burden on speech in violation of First Amendment. District court granted summary judgment to government on both claims. D.C. Circuit reversed on Fifth Amendment claim, holding that Section 407 as applied by Copyright Office in this case was unconstitutional. This was taking because exchange was not voluntary and plaintiff did not receive valuable government benefit from exchange, as mandatory deposit is not required to secure benefit of copyright. This is distinct from Section 408, through which owners may deposit works along with application and filing fee to obtain copyright registration, with registration serving as government benefit to copyright owner. Though Office argued that there was no taking because plaintiff had option of disavowing copyright protection, that option was never made known in any regulation, guidance, or communication, and was first mentioned in this litigation.

Wilder v. Hoiland, No. 22-1254, 2024 U.S. Dist. LEXIS 18051 (S.D.N.Y. Feb. 1, 2024)

District court denied plaintiff's motion for summary judgment, holding that factual record was inconclusive as to plaintiff's alleged ownership of copyright in work at issue. Plaintiff Esther Wilder, faculty member at City University of New York, sued another CUNY faculty member, Sarah Hoiland, for alleged infringement of plaintiff's written materials focused on assisting educators in developing assessment plans and instruction for measuring success of infusing numeracy and quantitative reasoning in classrooms ("Unit 7H"). Plaintiff prepared Unit 7H as part of faculty development program entitled NICHE, which was funded by National Science Foundation grant. In February 2019, defendant Hoiland attended educational conference and presented slides containing portions of text of Unit 7H. Defendant did not include plaintiff's name in slides, but claimed to have orally referenced plaintiff numerous times during presentation. Plaintiff obtained copy of defendant's presentation, then registered copyright in Unit 7H materials in April 2021 and subsequently filed suit. In reviewing plaintiff's motion for summary judgment, district court first noted that it would give plaintiff's registration only minor evidentiary weight, because plaintiff registered Unit 7H two years after alleged infringement, and more than five years after Unit 7H was first published. Regarding ownership, district court held that factual record precluded summary judgment, in part because NSF materials identified CUNY as recipient of grant money, and stated that grantee retained copyright in works. Finally, Unit 7H materials contained copyright notice stating that (a) materials were owned by CUNY and NICHE and (b) questions regarding authorization for use of materials were to be directed to plaintiff. District court therefore held that record evidence did not establish as matter of law that plaintiff owned copyright in Unit 7H materials.

> *Trent P. Fisher Enters., LLC v. SAS Automation, LLC*, No. 20-216, 2023 U.S. Dist. LEXIS 135933 (S.D. Ohio Aug. 3, 2023)

District court denied defendants' motion for summary judgment on plaintiffs' infringement claim. Plaintiffs, Trent P. Fisher Enterprises, LLC ("Fisher Enterprises") and Fisher Family Dynasty Trust ("Fisher Trust"), sold defendant SAS to defendants Piab USA, Inc. and Piab AB. As part of transaction, Fisher transferred equity in SAS to Piab, but Piab assigned IP rights in SAS's proprietary e-commerce software ("Works") to Fisher to be licensed back to Piab. Works were developed in significant part with code from open-source e-commerce software OpenCart pursuant to GNU General Public License ("GPL"), obliging developers to publicly disclose source code and make work available for free use if software developed via GPL is "covered work" and "conveyed" to third party. When Piab developed in-house e-commerce software largely based on source code from Works, plaintiffs sued alleging copyright infringement. Defendants moved for summary judgment on basis that Fisher did not own valid copyright in Works because no assignment of record showed Fisher Trust, which was assigned Works by SAS, transferring Works to licensing entity Fisher Enterprises. As Fisher Enterprises registered copyrights within five years of completion of Works, court found Fisher Enterprises entitled to presumption of validity, and that defendants bore burden to overcome presumption with evidence that Works were never assigned to Fisher Enterprises. Since defendants could produce no such evidence, court denied defendants' motion for summary judgment.

IV. FORMALITIES

A. Registration

> *Enter. Mgmt. Ltd., Inc. v. Construx Software Builders, Inc.*, 73 F.4th 1048 (9th Cir. 2023)

Ninth Circuit reversed district court's grant of summary judgment, vacated jury verdict, and held that by registering derivative work, author registers all material included in derivative work, including that which previously appeared in unregistered, original work created by author. Plaintiff sued defendant for infringement for copying chart. Defendant argued that evidence did not show he copied registered work because chart was not included in registration certificate. Jury returned verdict for defendant and plaintiff appealed. Ninth Circuit reiterated holding in *Unicolors v. H&M*, whereby Supreme Court held that Act provides safe harbor for inaccurate information in registration certificate such that certificate is valid even if it contains inaccurate information unless applicant included information with knowledge it was inaccurate and inaccuracy of information, if known, would have caused refusal of registration. Defendant did not argue plaintiff knowingly omitted information about preexisting works or that information about preexisting works was material. Even if plaintiff was not entitled to safe harbor for inaccurate information in registration certificate, registration certificate accurately stated it registered derivative work. Court found genuine issue of material fact whether plaintiff registered chart by including it in material corresponding to registration certificate. Court reversed grant of summary judgment for defendant and vacated jury verdict. Additionally, district court instructed jury that if it found defendant "accessed and copied other work but did not copy the registered work then the challenged work is an independent creation," and jury verdict should be for defendant. Ninth Circuit concluded instructions were incorrect because if elements in original work were copied in infringing work, and defendant copied elements in infringing work, defendant's copy infringed original work. Court found incorrect instruction was not harmless because it allowed jury to find in favor of defendant even if chart infringed plaintiff's copyright.

Philpot v. Indep. J. Review, 92 F.4th 252 (4th Cir. 2024)

Reversing district court's holding, Fourth Circuit held that defendant's alternative defense of invalid registration was not established. Plaintiff, photographer Larry Philpot, alleged that defendant Independent Journal Review ("IJR") infringed his photograph of musician Ted Nugent in online article. Defendant moved for summary judgment on basis that plaintiff's registration was invalid. District court found issue of fact regarding valid registration. Defendant argued that plaintiff improperly filed photo for registration in group of unpublished works when in fact it was already published, because plaintiff had entered into license agreement with third party AXS TV to distribute photo. District court found issue of fact regarding whether publication occurred when plaintiff entered agreement or delivered photo to third party. Fourth Circuit held dispute was of law, not fact, because relevant question was whether agreement with AXS TV constituted offer of distribution constituting publication under Act. Applying agreement's choice of California law, Fourth Circuit held that agreement's plain language made clear that upon delivery of one thousand of plaintiff's photos, plaintiff would grant license to AXS TV only for purpose of reviewing and examining photos and selecting twelve photos for curation. Prior to selection, AXS TV was expressly prohibited from displaying plaintiff's photos. Only upon selection of twelve photos would plaintiff then send high-resolution copies of photos to AXS TV and grant it license to reproduce photos. Fourth Circuit therefore concluded that plaintiff did not intend to distribute subject work by signing agreement with AXS TV, nor did it offer to do so. Defendant's defense of invalid registration was accordingly rejected.

Wozniak v. Warner Bros. Ent. Inc., No. 22-8969, 2024 U.S. Dist. LEXIS 55146 (S.D.N.Y. Mar. 27, 2024)

District court held, on summary judgment, that defendants owned valid copyright registrations relating to Batman universe, but that plaintiff did not own valid copyright registration for his unauthorized derivative work. Since publishing first Batman story in 1939, third-party defendant DC Comics and its predecessors-in-interest had published countless works depicting Batman universe and had obtained thousands of copyright registrations for Batman works. Between 1985 and 1999, plaintiff, writer and illustrator, created freelance artwork for DC Comics pursuant to agreements in which he acknowledged that his artwork would be derivative of preexisting material to which he would have no claim. In 1990, plaintiff wrote story eventually titled "The Blind Man's Hat" ("Story"), which featured aging Batman solving six puzzles arranged by Riddler while viral plague causes China to go into quarantine. At one point, Batman mistakenly believes that Riddler has uncovered his true identity of Bruce Wayne. In final trial, Riddler reveals he created virus to precipitate Armageddon, but Batman retrieves antidote and saves humanity. Between 1990 and 1999, plaintiff pitched Story to four DC Comics editors but they all rejected it. In 2017, defendant Warner Bros., DC Comics' licensee, set out to create new Batman movie called *The Batman*, screenplay for which was independently written by Matt Reeves without contact with, or creative contribution from, DC Comics. Released in 2022, *The Batman* depicted younger Batman facing off against Riddler, who murdered prominent Gotham citizens while leaving cryptic clues. At one point, Batman mistakenly believes that Riddler has uncovered his true identity of Bruce Wayne. Meanwhile, Riddler radicalizes his social media followers and attempts to assassinate Gotham's mayor before being defeated by Batman. After viewing *The Batman* in 2022, plaintiff obtained registration for Story. After plaintiff sued Warner Bros. for copyright infringement, DC Comics intervened and countersued for, *inter alia*, copyright infringement. Plaintiff argued that DC Comics—despite adducing large representative sample from thousands of copyright registrations covering Batman universe works—had failed to create rebuttable presumption of valid ownership of copyright therein because DC Comics had not come forward with agreement showing that Batman's original individual creators had assigned copyrights in Batman characters to DC Comics. Court held that, because plaintiff had not adduced any evidence casting doubt on validity of DC Comics' claim of ownership of original Batman works, DC Comics was not required to prove original assignment. Plaintiff also challenged validity of DC Comics' copyright registrations by pointing out that some of them were registered under separate entities, but court held this was irrelevant where DC Comics' witnesses had, without refutation, testified that these entities were DC Comics' predecessors-in-interest. Further, court held that it was plaintiff who did not have valid copyright registration. As preliminary matter, it was unclear that plaintiff could invoke rebuttable presumption of validity based on registration because there was no evidence that Story had ever been published, let alone within five years of registration. Even if plaintiff's registration was presumed valid *arguendo*, Warner Bros. had successfully rebutted that presumption because Story was unauthorized derivative work where plaintiff had conceded that Story represented reimagining of Batman universe whose entire premise centers on Batman. Accordingly, DC Comics owned valid copyright registrations but plaintiff did not.

Elohim Epf United States, Inc. v. 162 D & y Corp., No. 19-2431, 2023 U.S. Dist. LEXIS 224891 (S.D.N.Y. Dec. 18, 2023)

District court held that plaintiff's group registrations valid despite some evidence that individual compositions may have been published earlier. Non-party songwriter Brave Brother assigned to non-party Elohim Korea exclusive rights to administer certain Korean-language compositions. Elohim Korea, pursuant to subpublishing agreement, assigned to plaintiff Elohim USA exclusive rights to administer compositions in United States. Plaintiff registered compositions, including seven disputed works at issue in case, before suing defendants, karaoke establishments, for infringing plaintiff's public performance rights. Defendants urged that exhibit to subpublishing agreement, as well as public records maintained by Korean Music Copyright Association ("KOMCA"), collective copyright administration non-profit, showed that five of seven disputed works had been published prior to being published as part of "single unit of publication" identified in their respective registration certificate. Court characterized this evidence as "thin" and noted that defendants did not identify how, when and where compositions were previously published nor introduce documentary or testimonial evidence of works' earlier publication. Without such context or supporting evidence, dates in subpublishing agreement and KOMCA records did not defeat presumption of registrations' validity.

Laatz v. Zazzle, Inc., No. 22-4844, 2024 U.S. Dist. LEXIS 40600 (N.D. Cal. Mar. 7, 2024)

District court denied plaintiff's motion to dismiss counterclaim seeking declaration of invalidity of copyrights in plaintiff's fonts which formed basis of her claim. Plaintiff alleged that defendants, operators of online design platform Zazzle, fraudulently obtained license to use software containing three fonts created by plaintiff, and violated license by making fonts available to millions of people on Zazzle platform, including for commercial use. Defendant counterclaimed that plaintiff's copyright registrations were invalid, alleging that plaintiff did not actually write code in computer files she registered, and that third party application actually generated code. Copyright examiner had told plaintiff that she could not obtain registration if code was not hand-coded by human, and after twice responding in ways that neither confirmed nor denied that code was hand-coded, plaintiff finally stated that she hand-coded code. Initially, court did not make finding requested by plaintiff that Copyright Office was legally required to issue registrations, finding that disputed issues of fact about authorship prevented such determination. Despite disputed facts about who produced code, defendant's well-pleaded allegations that plaintiff was not author of code must be accepted on motion to dismiss counterclaim, and defendant thus adequately pleaded that plaintiff made knowing misrepresentations in copyright applications that should have precluded registration.

Alkam Home Fashion, Inc. v. Decor, No. 23-1177, 2023 U.S. Dist. LEXIS 169612 (C.D. Cal. Sept. 22, 2023)

District court dismissed plaintiff's complaint without prejudice. Plaintiff and defendant both engaged in development, sale, and marketing of linen design products; plaintiff alleged infringement of its copyrighted linen designs. In motion to dismiss, defendant alleged that plaintiff failed to establish ownership of valid copyright in designs at issue, by providing evidence of copyright registrations for photographs of textile designs rather than textile designs themselves. Plaintiff argued in response that registrations constituted *prima facie* evidence of copyright validity. District court agreed that plaintiff's registrations covered photographic works, not textile designs, and therefore dismissed complaint without prejudice, noting that failure to file amended complaint would result in dismissal with prejudice.

Thaler v. Perlmutter, No. 22-1564, 2023 U.S. Dist. LEXIS 145823 (D.D.C. Aug. 18, 2023)

District court granted motion for summary judgment filed by defendant Register of Copyrights, affirming Register's refusal to register visual artwork generated by plaintiff's AI computer system, "Creativity Machine," on basis that work failed to meet human authorship requirement for copyright registration. Sole issue was "whether a work generated entirely by an artificial system absent human involvement should be eligible for copyright"; court agreed with defendants that "human authorship is an essential part of a valid copyright claim." Plaintiff's copyright application stated that work was "autonomously created by a computer algorithm running on a machine," and claimed copyright ownership "as a work-for-hire to the owner of" machine. Court stated that while "copyright law has proven malleable enough to cover works created with or involving technologies developed long after traditional media of writing memorialized on paper," human authorship requirement is established by plain text of Copyright Act and judicial and legislative history of interpretation of copyright law. Plaintiff was unable to point to case in which "a court has recognized copyright in a work originating with a non-human." Plaintiff argued Creativity Machine was "entirely controlled" by him and "the AI only operates at [his] direction," but court found administrative record at Copyright Office included no such claim, so court must operate on presumption work created absent any human involvement. Court held Register properly denied registration due to absence of human authorship.

Richardson v. Kharbouch, No. 19-2321, 2024 U.S. Dist. LEXIS 1815 (N.D. Ill. Jan. 4, 2024)

District court concluded defendant entitled to judgment as matter of law where plaintiff failed to create triable issue of fact on infringement of his sound recording. Parties came before court second time on summary judgment to address issues largely ignored on first round of briefing. Plaintiff music producer sued defendant hip-hop artist, bringing claims defendant infringed his own original music recording "Hood Pushin' Weight" ("HPW") with defendant's song "Ain't Worried About Nothin'" ("AWAN"). In 2012, plaintiff composed HPW at age 16, and posted it to SoundClick.com. Six months later, defendant released AWAN, which immediately became immensely popular on Billboard charts. Defendant admitted he contributed to AWAN by writing lyrics, but stated underlying music was created by others. Plaintiff failed to develop record on this point and did not depose any of defendant's producers. On hearing AWAN in 2013, plaintiff formed opinion that AWAN's underlying beat copied certain aspects of HPW. Over next several years, defendant performed AWAN hundreds of times. Plaintiff eventually brought suit in 2021. Main issue before court was fact that plaintiff's registration only covered sound recording of HPW, and he thus had more limited protection for his work than if he also had registration for musical composition. Copyright registration for sound recording covers recording itself, but not underlying music, lyrics, words or other content. Rights in sound recording do not extend to "sound-alike" works merely imitating, but not duplicating, recording itself. Plaintiff failed to provide evidence supporting reasonable inference that HPW's actual sounds were physically duplicated. Plaintiff asserted defendant directly sampled HPW but cited no evidence in record beyond assertions that sampling common in hip-hop music industry and that "any jury" would be able to hear that AWAN sampled HPW. Plaintiff also put forth no evidence that defendant's live performances were done by digital audio transmission. Court agreed with defendant that plaintiff's evidence of any similarities in melody between AWAN and HPW was irrelevant and that evidence that any portion of actual sound recording of HPW itself had been misappropriated was absent.

Dmarcian, Inc. v. DMARC Advisor BV, No. 21-67, 2023 U.S. Dist. LEXIS 102010 (W.D.N.C. June 12, 2023)

District court referred to Register of Copyrights question of whether registration would have issued if inaccuracies regarding year of completion and publication date were known.

Plaintiff brought infringement claim against its former CEO regarding anti-phishing software owned by plaintiff. In 2021, plaintiff filed application for and obtained registration of source code, stating that work was completed and published in United States in 2012. Registration issued in 2021. In 2022, plaintiff submitted supplemental application to correct author of work from plaintiff to defendant, asserting that work was authored by defendant and then transferred to plaintiff. Code submitted in application was excerpted from larger work finished between 2017 and 2021, on which nine additional developers also worked. After parties fell out and plaintiff sued, defendant argued that supplemental application was inaccurate with respect to authorship, but court found that defendant provided no basis to find that other nine developers contributed copyrightable elements to work. Defendant also argued that application was inaccurate with respect to year. Though plaintiff argued that work evolved from code originally started in 2012, court found that because code was fixed in completed form in 2021, and 2021 version was submitted with application—not alleged 2012 version—work was completed in 2021. Court concluded that plaintiff knowingly put incorrect year on application, and referred to Register question whether it would have refused registration if it had known code was created and published in or after 2017, and specific code submitted in deposit copy was created in 2021.

Oliver v. Meow Wolf, Inc., No. 20-237, 2023 U.S. Dist. LEXIS 114812 (D.N.M. July 5, 2023)

District court granted defendants' motion to invalidate plaintiff's copyright registration and exclude plaintiff's affidavit submitted with reply brief; district court also denied plaintiff's motion to allow supplementary copyright application to proceed while litigation is pending. Plaintiff alleged infringement of her visual work entitled Ice Station Quellette, which included artwork, sculpture, text, and photographs, and was housed in permanent exhibition at House of Eternal Return (HER), which was operated by defendant Meow Wolf, Inc. (Meow). Plaintiff sued Meow and its former CEO, alleging, *inter alia*, infringement of two of plaintiff's registered copyrights (one nondramatic literary work (TX) and one visual arts work (VA)). Meow counterclaimed for declaratory judgment sounding in contract. In connection with VA registration, plaintiff submitted deposit copy of artistic bench, and listed herself as sole author of work, but later admitted that another artist had designed bench. Copyright Office stated that it would have refused VA registration if it had known plaintiff was not author of artistic bench, but noted plaintiff could correct deficiency with supplementary registration once litigation concluded. In evaluating parties' motions, district court concluded that safe harbor provision of Section 411(b) did not apply and VA registration was therefore invalid, including because: plaintiff knowingly and inaccurately listed herself as sole author; she presented new evidence in reply brief that did not create genuine issue of material fact regarding knowledge and inaccuracy of authorship listed on application; and she failed to present any evidence or argument to overcome conclusion that Register would have refused registration if it had known of inaccuracy. Though Register had indicated that inaccuracy could be corrected via supplementary application, district court held that plaintiff's anticipated change to registration was not minor, and for that reason and totality of circumstances—including potential confusion, complication, delay in litigation, or prejudice to defendant—district court refused to allow plaintiff to file supplementary registration application.

Covetrus Inc. v. Actian Corp., No. 21-97, 2023 U.S. Dist. LEXIS 176646 (D. Me. Oct. 2, 2023)

District court denied plaintiff's motion to refer to Register of Copyright questions relating to errors in application for one of defendant's registration certificates. Plaintiff brought action for declaratory judgment regarding scope of plaintiff's license to use defendant's data integration software. Defendant counterclaimed for breach of license and copyright infringement. Plaintiff argued one of defendant's copyright registrations should be invalidated, due in part to misstatements in application and inclusion of third-party code in deposit copy. To remedy, defendant sought supplemental registrations for Work. Plaintiff filed motion to refer questions to Register of Copyright to determine whether inaccurate information in application and deposit copy, if known at time of registration, would have resulted in refusal of registration. Court noted registrants are also authorized to file applications for supplemental registration to correct errors in registrations in such situations. Court allowed defendant leave to supplement registrations, noting that multiple other registrations relating to work had already issued, so invalidation of registration in question would not significantly affect outcome, and supplementation would promote "economic and speedy disposition" of controversy, while plaintiff's proposed referral to Copyright Office would further delay matter.

V. INFRINGEMENT

A. Access

Johnston v. Kroeger, No. 23-5024, 2024 U.S. App. LEXIS 3806 (5th Cir. Feb. 19, 2024)

Fifth Circuit affirmed dismissal of infringement suit in which plaintiff alleged that Nickelback copied his song. Plaintiff songwriter alleged that popular band Nickelback's hit 2005 song *Rockstar* infringed plaintiff's 2000 song *Rock Star*. District court dismissed claim on summary judgment, and Fifth Circuit agreed. Because plaintiff lacked direct evidence of copying, he attempted to satisfy factual copying element of his copyright claim by means of circumstantial evidence that defendants had access to plaintiff's work and that there was "probative similarity" between defendants' and plaintiff's works. Fifth Circuit found that plaintiff's theories of access—including Nickelback's record label and management group possibly attending Snowblind shows and two bands "moving in relatively the same circles" when looking for record labels—were speculative and required "'leaps of logic' that [were] not supported by the record." Absent factual copying plaintiff was required to prove striking similarity, which he could not do.

> *Ronk v. Hudson*, No. 20-9843, 2023 U.S. Dist. LEXIS 204089 (C.D. Cal. Nov. 13, 2023)

District court granted motion to dismiss infringement claim where complaint failed to allege access to or copying of plaintiff's song. Defendants argued that plaintiff did not allege plausible theory by which defendants could have obtained access to lyrics of plaintiff's song. Plaintiff argued that Ninth Circuit has held that access may be established by trivial showing that work is available on demand. Court found this to be misreading of precedent which would mean that any song ever uploaded to internet meets test for access. Allegation that one defendant has commented that she has "creeped" on other artists' profiles was not specific allegation that defendants looked at plaintiff's song specifically.

> *Antony v. Buena Vista Books, Inc.*, No. 18-205, 2024 U.S. Dist. LEXIS 9918 (E.D. Ky. Jan. 19, 2024)

District court granted summary judgment dismissing plaintiff's claim that young adult books published by Disney infringed his Zodiac-themed screenplay. Plaintiff, inspired by Chinese restaurant placemat, wrote screenplay about 12 children with powers themed after animals in Chinese Zodiac. Plaintiff then met and left copies of screenplay with multiple representatives of entertainment companies, allegedly including Disney representative, at 2006 Screenwriting Expo in Los Angeles. After Disney's publishing arm released book series in which children gain Zodiac-themed powers, plaintiff filed infringement claim. Though court denied motion to dismiss, it rejected plaintiff's claim on summary judgment. Court found that plaintiff failed to prove he had given copy of screenplay to Disney representative. He did not remember name of person he gave it to, and only remembered vague physical features. He later performed online searches for websites associated with pitch festivals and found particular person he thought he gave it to, but she submitted declaration saying she had not been employed by Disney since 1993, and plaintiff later admitted he was not sure it was her. Court found that even if he had given copy to Disney representative, there was no proof of nexus between that recipient and creators of book series.

B. Copying and Substantial Similarity

Johnston v. Kroeger, No. 23-5024, 2024 U.S. App. LEXIS 3806 (5th Cir. Feb. 19, 2024)

Fifth Circuit affirmed dismissal of infringement suit in which plaintiff alleged that Nickelback copied his song. Plaintiff songwriter alleged that popular band Nickelback's hit 2005 song *Rockstar* infringed plaintiff's 2000 song *Rock Star*. District court dismissed claim on summary judgment, and Fifth Circuit agreed. Plaintiff argued that district court erred by not applying "more discerning ordinary observer test," but Fifth Circuit disagreed, as that standard is used in some substantial similarity analyses, which occur after plaintiff has established factual copying. Absent evidence of factual copying, courts require striking similarity. Court found that similarities were not so great as to preclude all explanations but copying, as many of Nickelback's works and other rock songs had same similarities. Similar categories of lyrics, such as "making lots of money," "connections to famous people," and "references to sports" were common musical clichés. Moreover, "reference to sports" category overstated similarities between works: plaintiff wrote about potentially buying Dallas Cowboys football team while Nickelback's work contained line about having bathroom big enough in which to play baseball.

Wozniak v. Warner Bros. Ent. Inc., No. 22-8969, 2024 U.S. Dist. LEXIS 55146 (S.D.N.Y. Mar. 27, 2024)

District court held, on summary judgment, that defendants had established unauthorized copying but plaintiff had not. Since publishing first Batman story in 1939, third-party defendant DC Comics and its predecessors-in-interest had published countless works depicting Batman universe and had obtained thousands of copyright registrations for Batman works. Between 1985 and 1999, plaintiff, writer and illustrator, created freelance artwork for DC Comics pursuant to agreements in which he acknowledged that his artwork would be derivative of preexisting material to which he would have no claim. In 1990, plaintiff wrote story eventually titled "The Blind Man's Hat" ("Story"), which featured aging Batman solving six puzzles arranged by Riddler while viral plague causes China to go into quarantine. At one point, Batman mistakenly believes that Riddler has uncovered his true identity of Bruce Wayne. In final trial, Riddler reveals he created virus to precipitate Armageddon but Batman retrieves antidote and saves humanity. Between 1990 and 1999, plaintiff pitched Story to four DC Comics editors but they all rejected it. In 2008, plaintiff submitted Story to individual named Michael Uslan, who was listed as executive producer on Batman media due to 1979 option that Uslan had acquired to depict Batman characters in film. However, despite his EP credit, Uslan was not involved in development or creation of those films. In 2017, defendant Warner Bros., DC Comics' licensee, set out to create new Batman movie called *The Batman*, screenplay for which was independently written by Matt Reeves without contact with, or creative contribution from, DC Comics. Released in 2022, *The Batman* depicted younger Batman facing off against Riddler, who murdered prominent Gotham citizens while leaving cryptic clues. At one point, Batman mistakenly believes that Riddler has uncovered his true identity of Bruce Wayne. Meanwhile, Riddler radicalizes his social media followers and attempts to assassinate Gotham's mayor before being defeated by Batman. After viewing *The Batman* in 2022, plaintiff obtained registration for Story. After plaintiff sued Warner Bros. for copyright infringement, DC Comics intervened and countersued for, *inter alia*, copyright infringement. Court held that DC Comics had established both actual copying and substantial similarity as to plaintiff's Story because plaintiff conceded he had intentionally created Story by exploiting Batman characters and story elements, and had hoped it would be published as part of Batman comic book series. Even high-level review of Story revealed that characters were not merely substantially similar to, but were, in fact, Batman universe characters. Plaintiff argued that his copying was with DC Comics' consent but, at most, DC Comics consented to such copying for limited purpose of pitching artwork or scripts to DC Comics itself. Moreover, for artwork plaintiff had successfully sold to DC Comics, plaintiff had signed agreements acknowledging that DC Comics owned all rights in preexisting Batman universe material, and there was no evidence plaintiff had received authorization from DC Comics to exploit any Batman universe story for his own personal use. Court further held that plaintiff had failed to establish either access or substantial similarity in support of his own copyright infringement claim. Chain of events alleged by plaintiff as leading to access was no more than theoretically possible. No copies of Story were found at Warner Bros. or DC Comics, nor was there evidence that anyone at DC Comics had read, discussed or retained Story, let alone taken any steps to furnish it to Warner Bros. Also, Reeves attested that he never had never seen or heard of Story or Wozniak before writing "The Batman," did not have contact with DC Comics while writing screenplay, and had conceived of "The Batman" plot on his own. As for Uslan, undisputed evidence showed that only reason he was identified as executive producer was due to long-ago agreement with Warner Bros. requiring that he be so credited on any film involving Batman characters. After filtering out Story's unprotectable elements—which eliminated those referencing any elements from Batman universe—only four ostensible similarities remained between Story and "The Batman" and none of these could support substantial similarity claim. Serial killer portrayed as loner was standard, if not hackneyed, trope, while villain attempting to get revenge on society by precipitating its destruction is common plot feature (and chosen means of destruction differed between Story and *The Batman*). Likewise, villain's moment of epiphany that leads him to life of crime or subsequent taunting of pursuers by leaving series of riddles were both quotidian thematic concepts. Accordingly, DC Comics had established unauthorized copying of copyrighted material but plaintiff had not.

Davis v. ABC, No. 22-5944, 2024 U.S. Dist. LEXIS 48187 (S.D.N.Y. Mar. 19, 2024)

District court granted defendants' motions to dismiss for failure to state claim where plaintiff failed to establish substantial similarity between her television script and ABC show *Abbott Elementary*. Plaintiff public school teacher and writer authored television script *This School Year* ("*TSY*") based on personal experience as teacher. In March 2020, plaintiff registered *TSY* with Copyright Office. Mid-2020, plaintiff began working with defendant production company ("BPP Defendants") to bring *TSY* to market, including signing NDA and corresponding about script. Plaintiff was told BPP Defendants would help present *TSY* to major outlets such as Hulu and ABC. BPP Defendants gave plaintiff notes on script, which plaintiff incorporated, but at some point, during 2020, BPP Defendants stopped responding. Show *Abbott Elementary* was pitched to ABC by actor Quinta Brunson (together, "Abbott Defendants" along with other individuals connected to show) in late 2020, and pilot aired following year. Both *TSY* and *Abbott Elementary* are mockumentary-style workplace comedies taking place in public schools (NYC and Philadelphia, respectively). Court agreed with defendants, who argued that any similarities identified by plaintiff either had their root in common and unprotectible elements that could not support copyright claim or were not actually similar at all, evidenced by discerning ordinary observer's consideration of both works. Court found plot and themes appreciably different. As threshold matter, plaintiff's suggestion that both protagonists attempt to "survive and thrive in their chosen professions" is generalized idea that is not copyrightable. Differences in plot structure and subplots outweigh general similarities. Further, characters in both works were dissimilar although plaintiff was technically correct that both works have "young, African American female lead characters." Characters had different attitudes toward profession of teaching. Finally, remaining cast of characters were distinct, and stock tensions among these characters were simply *scènes à faire* in workplace comedies. Court found minor similarities in setting, format, and pace could not support plaintiff's infringement claim and that total concept and overall feel of works appreciably different. Therefore, court granted defendants' motions to dismiss for failure to state claim.

Peabody & Co. LLC v. Wayne, No. 22-10316, 2024 U.S. Dist. LEXIS 24268 (S.D.N.Y. Feb. 12, 2024)

District court dismissed copyright infringement claim because asserted elements of plaintiff's composition were not protectable and because parties' works not substantially similar. Plaintiff, owner of composition for "Come On Down," claimed that Roddy Ricch's song "The Box" infringed plaintiff's copyright. Court held that, under ordinary observer test, no reasonable jury could find works were substantially similar, because "Come On Down" was soul song with melodic tune, while "The Box" was hip-hop song delivered in monotone rap. Plaintiff could still state copyright infringement claim based on fragmented literal similarity test if it could show that defendants copied protectable portion of plaintiff's composition "exactly or nearly exactly." However, plaintiff failed under this test as well because composition's individual elements—glissando and repeated two-chord progression, appearing in particular order and played on instrumental set of violin, synthesizer keyboard, electric bass and drum set with particular tone setting—were not protectable as matter of law. Because plaintiff pointed to only five eligible elements through parties' respective songs, asserted elements were not numerous enough for selection-and-arrangement claim. Finally, plaintiff had failed to allege that "The Box" in fact copied important features of composition, because plaintiff's "signature instrumental melodic figure" was expressed differently in defendant's song.

State Street Global Advisors Tr. Co. v. Visbal, 677 F. Supp. 3d 209 (S.D.N.Y. 2023)

District court granted defendant summary judgment on plaintiff's direct copyright infringement claim. Plaintiff, asset management company, hired defendant, sculptor, to sculpt what eventually became "Fearless Girl" statue (in which defendant registered copyright). After statue went viral, parties entered into series of contracts governing copyright ownership, pursuant to which defendant granted plaintiff exclusive copyright right in multiple areas, including use of statue in connection with gender diversity issues in corporate governance and financial services sector. Defendant, through her website, sold mini-replica of statute to individual executive at Edward Jones, financial services company, in 2018. In February 2019, unbeknownst to defendant, executive chose to place purchased replica in Edward Jones atrium for one morning during women's conference. Plaintiff sued defendant for direct copyright infringement. Court granted defendant's motion for summary judgment because defendant did not take any action to display or distribute replica of statue sold to Edward Jones executive.

Lee v. Warner Media, LLC, No. 23-6025, 2023 U.S. Dist. LEXIS 211437 (W.D.N.Y. Nov. 28, 2023)

District court granted defendants' motion to dismiss because court concluded no ordinary lay observer could find parties' works substantially similar beyond level of generalized or otherwise unprotectible ideas. Plaintiff alleged defendants' shows "Living Single," "Friends," "Sex and the City," and "Girlfriends" infringed copyright she held in "Girlfriends © 1991," which included copyrighted treatment and script of pilot episode "Sasha Says." Plaintiff alleged shows copied concept of having cast of urban characters living in urban building and everything that flows from premise. Court determined total concept and feel of works were different. Court found shows' theme, setting, characters, time sequence, plot, and pace not substantially similar. Court found plot elements in shows completely different, and alleged similarities too generalized. Court determined while elements are present in shows, actual plot of each show was different and go in different direction. Court held no substantial similarity between shows because not similar in mood, details, or characterization, and even if there are any similarities, those similarities not protectible.

Hines v. BMG Rights Mgmt. (US) LLC, No. 20-3535, 2023 U.S. Dist. LEXIS 170372 (S.D.N.Y. Sept. 25, 2023)

District court granted defendants' motions for summary judgment. Plaintiff Ernie Hines sued defendants W Chappell Music Corporation, and artists Jay-Z, Timbaland, and Ginuwine for alleged use of three-bar guitar riff ("Introduction") at beginning of plaintiff's 1960s composition "Help Me Put Out The Flame (In My Heart)" in defendants' hip-hop songs "Paper Chase" and "Toe 2 Toe." District court first held that Introduction was ineligible for copyright protection, because it was drawn primarily from musical device found in 1914 public domain work "Mysterioso Pizzicato." In addition, even if plaintiff could establish protectability, plaintiff could not establish substantial similarity. District court evaluated works under fragmented literal similarity test, which looks to quantitative and qualitive significance of copied portion in relation to plaintiff's work as whole. First, shortness of Introduction—three-bar riff running for six seconds out of 192-second song—lacked quantitative significance. Second, Introduction was not repeated within plaintiff's work, nor was its melody related to other melodies in work; in fact, Introduction was not even included in original deposit copy and was only added later in supplemental registration. Plaintiff argued that defendants' works included all or nearly all of plaintiff's Introduction. However, test does not look to whether copied material constitutes substantial portion of infringing work, but rather whether copied matter constituted substantial portion of plaintiff's work. Though plaintiff also claimed that copied portion was qualitatively significant due to distinctive sound of specific guitar used, such element was specific to sound recording, in which plaintiff could not claim copyright.

Dreamtitle Publ'g, LLC v. Penguin Random House LLC, No. 22-7500, 2023 U.S. Dist. LEXIS 115127 (S.D.N.Y. July 5, 2023)

District court granted defendant's motion to dismiss. Plaintiff, author of book *I'm a Brilliant Little Black Boy*, alleged that defendant's book *I Am Every Good Thing* infringed its work. Plaintiff alleged that works were substantially similar because both shared common goal of promoting self-esteem of black children. In particular, both books were illustrated picture books, featured black boys as characters, included plot elements of boys playing basketball, wearing capes, participating in hip hop and science, and using some rhyming elements. Court found no substantial similarity since total look and feel of books were different. Further, court found many, if not all elements plaintiff claimed were similar to be *scènes à faire*, and thus not protectable.

Enos v. Walt Disney Co., No. 23-5790, 2024 U.S. Dist. LEXIS 39705 (C.D. Cal. Mar. 4, 2024)

District court denied defendants' motion to dismiss because plaintiff's character was copyrightable. Plaintiffs created Honu, Hawaiian sea turtle with blue eyes who plays ukulele, as part of songs, books, live theatrical performances, and other products. Defendants, collectively Disney, unveiled group of characters at Hawaiian resort that included Olu Mel, turtle with blue eyes who plays ukulele. Plaintiffs alleged that Disney illegally copied Honu in creating Olu and Disney moved to dismiss, arguing that Olu's differences outnumbered his similarities with Honu. Court denied motion because two original elements of Honu's character (blue eyes and musicality) are not stock and are present in Olu. Even though none of Honu's individual traits are protected, Honu protected as blue-eyed ukulele-playing turtle and plaintiff had sufficiently alleged that Onu substantially similar to that.

Simpson Strong-Tie Co. v. MiTek Inc., No. 20-6957, 2023 U.S. Dist. LEXIS 223876 (N.D. Cal. Dec. 15, 2023)

District court held that defendant's copying was *de minimis*. Plaintiff and defendant both designed, manufactured and sold construction products, and each published product catalogs. At issue were abbreviated part names (APIs) used in plaintiff's 2017-2018 and 2019-2020 copyrighted catalogs, each of which contained 20 or fewer new APIs, alphabetically listed alongside previously-included part names. Defendant copied APIs found in both catalogs and plaintiff sued for copyright infringement. Court held that plaintiff's rights extended only to new APIs and not material in earlier versions of catalogs. Although court found most APIs to contain minimal degree of creativity required for copyright protection, defendant's copying when viewed in comparison to entire catalogs was *de minimis* in terms of both quantity (12 APIs in list of 400) and quality (because APIs not source-identifying and indices in which they are located are essentially functional).

Tolkien Tr. v. Polychron, No. 23-4300, 2023 U.S. Dist. LEXIS 226135 (C.D. Cal. Dec. 14, 2023)

District court granted plaintiff's motion for summary judgment. Defendant Demetrious Polychron previously filed infringement claims against two Amazon companies, as well as entities and individual related to J.R.R. Tolkien estate. Polychron alleged Amazon and Tolkien estate had infringed his copyright in unauthorized derivative work *The Fellowship of the King* that was based on defendants' registered work. Amazon and Tolkien estate each filed motions to dismiss, which were granted. Subsequently, in present case, entities related to Tolkien estate filed infringement suit against Polychron, alleging that *The Fellowship of the King* infringed *The Lord of the Rings* by J.R.R. Tolkien. Tolkien plaintiffs moved for summary judgment against Polychron. District court found actual evidence of copying because defendant Polychron admitted to keeping his work as close as possible to *The Lord of the Rings* canon. Circumstantial evidence of copying also existed, as defendant admitted to reading and re-reading *The Lord of the Rings*, and his story allegedly copied characters and narratives from that work. Finally, district court found substantial similarity between plaintiffs' work and defendant's work. District court held that defense of independent creation was indefensible in light of how explicitly defendant stated that defendant's works were based on *The Lord of the Rings*. District court therefore granted plaintiffs' motion for summary judgment.

Sound & Color, LLC v. Smith, No. 22-1508, 2023 U.S. Dist. LEXIS 158043 (C.D. Cal. Sept. 6, 2023)

District court granted defendants' motion for summary judgment, finding plaintiff failed to establish genuine issue of material fact with respect to substantial similarity of plaintiff's song to defendant's song under extrinsic test. Plaintiff sued defendants for infringement of musical composition copyrights. Plaintiff claimed selection and arrangement of lyrics, pitch sequence, melodic contour, metric placement of syllables, rhythm, feel and structure sufficiently original to be protectable, and defendants' combination of elements substantially similar. Court held songs not substantially similar. Individual elements of song not individually protectable by copyright, including four-word phrase "dancing with a stranger." Court found pitch sequence and rhythm also not protectable. Court determined selection and arrangement copyright only available if otherwise unprotectable elements are numerous and original enough that combination constitutes original work of authorship. Court concluded defendants entitled to summary judgment on direct infringement claim and therefore, defendants also entitled to summary judgment on secondary infringement claims.

Elohim Epf United States, Inc. v. 600 N. Vt. Inc., No. 22-7516, 2023 U.S. Dist. LEXIS 127665 (C.D. Cal. June 15, 2023)

District court granted plaintiff's motion for summary judgment. Plaintiff sued defendants, karaoke establishments, for infringement for unauthorized public performance and public display of 18 musical compositions to which plaintiff had exclusive rights. Defendants argued that singing songs inside private rooms did not constitute public performance under Act. Defendants' establishments were open to public and charged patrons to rent private rooms to listen to songs for selection that included plaintiff's registered compositions. Court agreed with other Central District decisions that held karaoke performed in commercial karaoke establishments that are open to public constitute "public performance" under Act, regardless of whether karaoke is performed in private rooms. Court found karaoke establishments were unlike hotel rooms which provide privacy, but instead are like hotel meeting rooms, performance in which Ninth Circuit has held constitutes "public performance." Court determined defendants had not provided and could not provide evidence that they are not site of public performance.

> *Doorage, Inc. v. Blue Crates, LLC*, No. 20-421, 2023 U.S. Dist. LEXIS 170297 (N.D. Ill. Sep. 22, 2023)

District court granted summary judgment to plaintiff because parties' works were substantially similar. Plaintiff, door-to-door storage business, commissioned animated marketing videos describing its services and featuring plaintiff's logo and color scheme. Defendant, plaintiff's competitor, commissioned marketing videos expressly based on plaintiff's videos, which defendant sent to its vendor with instructions to "recreate" same. Defendant's resulting video was nearly identical to plaintiff's, using same style and formatting, same step-by-step instructions on use of company's services, and same background music, in nearly identical arrangement. When plaintiff moved for summary judgment on its copyright infringement claim, defendant invoked *scènes à faire* doctrine. Court held there was no question about actual copying, given defendant's instructions that its vendor create video at least modeled on plaintiff's and at most exact replica thereof. Moreover, even if general themes of plaintiff's video were not protectable, script, visual style and arrangement of defendant's video was minimally distinguishable from plaintiff's such that no reasonable person could differ as to videos' substantial similarity.

> *Widespread Elec. Sales, LLC v. Upstate Breaker Wholesale Supply, Inc.*, No. 20-2541, 2023 U.S. Dist. LEXIS 224054 (N.D. Tex. Dec. 17, 2023)

Court denied plaintiff's motion for summary judgment on defendant's liability for infringement where there was material fact question on substantial similarity. Founder of plaintiff company, seller of obscure and obsolete electrical products, created website in 2008. Founder chose products, arranged product pages with information (part number, product description and specifications, and photos), and spent "countless hours" typing product pages and creating database. To protect website and database, plaintiff applied for and received four Group Registrations for automated databases. Defendant company, also seller of electrical equipment, was founded in 2013. Defendant used scraping tool to copy text from plaintiff's website despite several anti-scraping and anti-spidering warnings on plaintiff's site. In 2020, plaintiff realized defendant had copied hundreds of thousands of plaintiff's product pages. Plaintiff sued for copyright infringement. Following close of discovery, both parties brought partial summary judgment motions. Court considered them together. Court found undisputed evidence that defendant copied plaintiff's works. Court next considered whether plaintiff showed substantial similarity between copyrighted works and defendant's allegedly infringing work. Defendant argued it copied only factual product information and arranged facts on its website differently than plaintiff's selection and arrangement, and that plaintiff could not show qualitative and quantitative similarity. Court reviewed side-by-side comparison and concluded that neither party satisfied summary judgment burden as to finding of infringement or noninfringement on plaintiff's copyright claim. There was evidence at least some portion of defendant's product pages were similar to protected elements of plaintiff's product pages, but similarities were not so overwhelming that court could find infringement as matter of law. Reasonable jurors could find for either party.

Fomo Factory, LLC v. Gallery Model Homes, Inc., No. 21-1022, 2023 U.S. Dist. LEXIS 130703 (S.D. Tex. July 28, 2023)

District court denied defendant's motion for summary judgment. Plaintiff alleged infringement of its "immersive art pop-ups," which provide visitors with opportunity to take photographs of themselves or others with creative backdrops and props. Kara Whitten was artist who assisted in creating works for plaintiff, and assigned her works and copyright to plaintiff. Furniture store defendant hired various artists, including Ms. Whitten, to design and install backdrop displays for its in-store furniture. Plaintiff alleged infringement of five copyrighted works, which contained pinwheels, seesaws, cupcakes, and fringes. On summary judgment motion, defendant argued that plaintiff failed to prove that defendant had copied plaintiff's copyrighted works. District court held access element of factual copying was satisfied, because plaintiff's works were created prior to defendant's works, and both sets of works were created by Ms. Whitten. Cursory review of side-by-side photographs of works revealed similarities in their use of themes, arrangements, sizes and proportions, decorative designs, and color schemes sufficient to support conclusion of appropriation. Though question of substantial similarity should usually be left for trial, exception exists in Fifth Circuit if no reasonable juror could find substantial similarity, or if copied portion of works are not original. District court held factual issues existed regarding originality. In addition, though defendant alleged its arrangement of similar items (e.g., seesaws and cupcakes) was distinguishable from plaintiff's arrangement, district court noted that Ms. Whitten had previously admitted that defendant's displays were similar to plaintiffs, but not exact, because she changed colors and dimensions. District court held that indefinite changes to colors and dimensions were insufficient to establish lack of similarity between works and insufficient to show that no reasonable juror could find substantial similarity. District court therefore denied defendant's motion for summary judgment.

Tecnoglass LLC v. Paredes, No. 22- 22356, 2023 U.S. Dist. LEXIS 116974 (S.D. Fla. July 6, 2023)

Plaintiff, manufacturer and owner of copyright in technical drawings relating to windows, sliding glass doors, and window wall systems for use in residential and construction industries, sued subcontractor for infringement, alleging defendant copied and used works as part of permit submissions for construction contracts.

On summary judgment, parties did not dispute plaintiff's ownership of copyrighted works or defendant's access to works, but defendant argued its works were not substantially similar. Defendants argued they never actually copied works, and disputed plaintiff's expert testimony on basis expert did not state that drawings were "identical" to plaintiff's, thus creating genuine issue of material fact as to copying. District court found mere argument that defendant did not copy works insufficient to create genuine issue of material fact, given clear evidence of access and substantial similarity. District court further rejected defendant's argument that plaintiff's expert report did not establish works were "identical," likewise pointing to substantial similarity standard and also to unrebutted language in expert testimony that works were "essentially identical" and "completely interchangeable." District court granted summary judgment to defendants on infringement.

Ambrosetti v. Or. Cath. Press, No. 21-211, 2024 U.S. Dist. LEXIS 45085 (D. Or. Mar. 13, 2024)

In case involving two pieces of Catholic liturgical music, district court agreed with magistrate judge that defendant was entitled to summary judgment on copyright infringement claim because plaintiff presented no admissible evidence showing defendant's access to plaintiff's work, and plaintiff did not show similarity between works. Court rejected magistrate judge's conclusion as to substantial similarity of works, holding there was substantial similarity under extrinsic test because works shared same key, meter, and verse, and shared same length and melodic phrases. However, court found similarities not so striking that they relieved plaintiff of burden to prove defendant's access to work because plaintiff's work began beat before defendant's did, and works varied rhythmically. Court held that if plaintiff were able to demonstrate defendant had access to work, then case would have presented triable issue on whether works substantially similar, but plaintiff did not show access or striking similarity, so court granted summary judgment to defendant.

Thomson Reuters Enter. Ctr. GmbH v. Ross Intel. Inc., No. 20-613, 2023 U.S. Dist. LEXIS 170155 (D. Del. Sept. 25, 2023)

District court denied parties' cross-motions for summary judgment. Plaintiff alleged defendant's AI software copied content from plaintiff's Westlaw legal research platform, as defendant's legal research contractor copied written content from Westlaw headnotes to be used as training data for defendant's AI software. Defendant's own expert admitted actual copying of at least 2,830 data sets. Plaintiff moved for summary judgment on infringement claim. Defendant argued copyright registration for works comprised "hundreds of thousands of headnotes and key numbers" so "copying a mere few thousand is not enough for infringement." Court rejected defendant's argument, as copying of specific wording of copyrightable components of compilation may comprise infringement. However, as parties disputed extent to which Westlaw required its attorney-editors to ensure works directly mirrored language of uncopyrightable judicial opinions, questions of fact remained. Court also stated that even if actual copying of works by defendant has been established as matter of law, question of substantial similarity must go to jury as parties disputed extent to which training data overlapped with works.

McFee v. Carolina Pad, LLC, No. 21-633, 2023 U.S. Dist. LEXIS 205753 (W.D.N.C. Nov. 16, 2023)

District court granted defendant's motion for summary judgment, determining that "no reasonable trier of fact would find substantial similarity … under the heightened standard that must be utilized for thin works." Plaintiff alleged copyright infringement by defendant, claiming defendant copied seven of plaintiff's print designs for use on back-to-school supplies. Court found that works, which consisted of common design elements in nature of "[p]olka dots, stripes and flowers," were entitled to only "thin" protection, stating that only particular arrangement of stripes, colors, and patterns, taken as whole, may perhaps be subject to protection, and only then, as "thin" copyright in which more than substantial similarity to allegedly infringing design must be shown. Upon comparison of works, court noted significant visual differences between plaintiff's works and allegedly infringing designs in terms of arrangement of polka dots, stripes, and flowers. As such, Court granted defendant's motion for summary judgment, finding plaintiff failed to establish specific, objective similarity, and plaintiff's arguments were insufficient to create genuine issue of material fact.

Critical Response Grp., Inc. v. Geo-Comm, Inc., No. 22-342, 2023 U.S. Dist. LEXIS 218414 (S.D. Iowa Nov. 20, 2023)

District court dismissed copyright infringement claims on summary judgment because defendant's maps not substantially similar to plaintiff's as matter of law. Plaintiff, maker of grid overlaid maps to assist first responders in emergency situations, had worked cooperatively with defendant, public safety geographic information systems company, to convert plaintiff's maps to different format. After parties' relationship became competitive, defendant had internal discussions about creating "carbon copy" of plaintiff's maps. Defendant eventually started making its own gridded maps, relying in part on plaintiff's maps but ultimately using different colors and more complicated labeling system. After plaintiff sued for copyright infringement, court found that, though defendant may have violated parties' license agreement, no infringement occurred. Plaintiff's maps were entitled to only thin copyright protection because their primary purpose was functional, much information therein came from other sources over which plaintiff did not claim copyright, and remainder of information consisted of non-copyrightable facts and ideas. Moreover, there was no substantial similarity between parties' respective maps due to differences in color schemes, x and y axis labeling conventions, stylization, arrows, text sizing, fonts, etc. and because maps were of entirely different locations in different states. Court granted summary judgment in defendant's favor notwithstanding defendant's employee's use of "carbon copy" in preliminarily describing what defendant's maps should look like.

Antony v. Buena Vista Books, Inc., No. 18-205, 2024 U.S. Dist. LEXIS 9918 (E.D. Ky. Jan. 19, 2024)

District court granted summary judgment dismissing plaintiff's claim that young adult books published by Disney infringed his Zodiac-themed screenplay. Plaintiff, inspired by Chinese Chinese restaurant placemat, wrote screenplay about 12 children with powers themed after animals in Chinese Zodiac. After Disney's publishing arm released book series in which children gain Zodiac-themed powers, plaintiff filed infringement claim. Though court denied motion to dismiss, it rejected plaintiff's claim on summary judgment. Court found that books were not substantially or strikingly similar to screenplay. Plaintiff conceded that simple idea of zodiac-powered superheroes is not protectible, and court found other common elements such as young superhero team in headquarters saving world while dealing with familiar issues were unprotectible stock themes. Court did not give credence to list plaintiff compiled of random similarities, finding that such lists are inherently subjective and unreliable. Ultimately, works were not similar beyond unprotectable or random elements. Plaintiff also failed to overcome evidence of independent creation by authors of books.

C. Contributory/Vicarious Infringement

Hunley v. Instagram, LLC, 73 F.4th 1060 (9th Cir. 2023)

Ninth Circuit affirmed that Instagram was not liable for secondary infringement when news platforms embedded plaintiffs' Instagram posts containing plaintiffs' photographs. Two photographers brought infringement claim against Instagram when third-party news sites published articles that contained embedded posts from photographers' Instagram pages. Embedding allows site to directly incorporate entire posts from sites such as Instagram, instructing browser to retrieve content from Instagram's server, as opposed to site pulling photographs from its own server. News sites that embedded posts in question did not store copies of underlying images. Applying "Server Test," district court and Ninth Circuit agreed that news sites, having not stored copies of photographs on their own servers, did not infringe, and without primary infringement by news sites, there could be no secondary infringement by Instagram.

Sony Music En., Inc. v. Cox Communs., Inc., 93 F.4th 222 (4th Cir. 2024)

Fourth Circuit affirmed in part and reversed in part, following jury verdict awarding $1 billion in statutory damages against internet service provider for vicarious liability and contributory infringement in connection with infringement of compositions and sound recordings by provider's subscribers. (Provider had previously been held ineligible for DMCA safe harbor under § 512 because its policy for terminating repeat infringers was inadequate.) As to vicarious liability, trial court had denied provider's motion for JMOL that it lacked sufficient "direct financial interest" for vicarious liability, but Circuit reversed and did not remand. Court acknowledged that financial interest could be sufficient "even absent a strict correlation between each act of infringement and an added penny of profits," such as where infringement draws more users to register with service, but plaintiffs failed to present evidence adequate to support reasonable inference of causal relationship between users' infringing activities and provider's financial benefit. "We therefore conclude that Cox is not vicariously liable." As to contributory infringement, district court had granted summary judgment to plaintiffs on knowledge element, and jury found for plaintiffs on element of material contribution. Circuit affirmed both results. As to knowledge, Court required that provider have knowledge that "infringement was substantially certain," and provider argued on appeal this was "a predictive question" that jury should have been allowed to resolve. Circuit disagreed, holding that provider had made no such argument in opposition to plaintiffs' summary judgment motion, and "did not even mention the 'substantially certain' standard" in its summary judgment briefing, so issue was not preserved for appeal. With respect to element of material contribution, Circuit affirmed jury's finding that provider "knew of specific instances of repeat copyright infringement" and "chose to continue providing [service] despite believing the online infringement would continue because it wanted to avoid losing revenue." Such evidence "was sufficient to support a finding that Cox materially contributed to copyright infringement."

State Street Global Advisors Tr. Co. v. Visbal, 677 F. Supp. 3d 209 (S.D.N.Y. 2023)

District court granted defendant summary judgment on plaintiff's vicarious infringement claim. Plaintiff, asset management company, hired defendant, sculptor, to sculpt what eventually became "Fearless Girl" statue (in which defendant registered copyright). After statue went viral, parties entered into series of contracts governing copyright ownership, pursuant to which defendant granted plaintiff exclusive copyright right in multiple areas, including use of statue in connection with gender diversity issues in corporate governance and financial services sector ("Gender Diversity Issues"). Defendant, through her website, sold mini-replica of statue to individual executive at Edward Jones, financial services company, in 2018. At time that executive purchased replica, defendant's website did not include language stating that (a) plaintiff's pre-approval was needed for purchase of replica by financial institution for any commercial or corporate purpose or (b) replicas could not be used in connection with Gender Diversity Issues. In February 2019, unbeknownst to defendant, executive chose to place purchased replica in Edward Jones atrium for one morning during women's conference. Plaintiff sued defendant for, *inter alia*, vicarious infringement. Court held that, because defendant was able to post (and later posted) disclaimers on her website reflecting restrictions on use of replicas, this established that defendant had right and ability to supervise and warn against any infringing activity. However, plaintiff failed to establish vicarious infringement because it did not show that plaintiff had direct financial interest in infringing activities. Edward Jones executive appeared to have purchased replica due to love of art and only later engaged in infringing activity (placing replica in atrium).

Lane Coder Photography, LLC v. Hearst Corp., No. 22-5071, 2023 U.S. Dist. LEXIS 159200 (S.D.N.Y. Sept. 8, 2023)

District court denied defendant Hearst's motion to dismiss plaintiff professional photographer's contributory infringement claim. Plaintiff was commissioned by Sotheby's to photograph Connecticut real estate "Greenacre." Pursuant to parties' agreement, Sotheby was to use photos for advertising property's sale and could not sub-license photos or transmit to other parties. Plaintiff obtained group copyright registration of photos. Shortly after, defendant Hearst Corporation published two online articles using several of plaintiff's photos without plaintiff's authorization—some with attribution to Sotheby's, some without. Defendant Yahoo published online article using at least one of plaintiff's photos with no attribution and informed plaintiff it received photos and content for article from defendant Hearst through content license agreement. Plaintiff did not authorize display or use of photos in articles and alleges defendant Hearst obtained photos from Sotheby's website and removed plaintiff's CMI. Defendant Hearst moved to dismiss contributory copyright infringement claim. Plaintiff alleged defendant engaged in contributory infringement when it distributed copies of photos to Yahoo pursuant to licensing agreement, thereby materially assisting in Yahoo's infringement. Primary issue court analyzed was extent of defendant's knowledge. Complaint alleged defendant's knowledge could be inferred from plaintiff's allegations that (1) Sotheby's did not provide photos to defendant or authorize defendant to use photos in its articles and (2) defendant improperly obtained photos through Sotheby's website. Court found these allegations sparse, but sufficient to permit court to infer defendant had reason to know photos were infringing when it provided them to Yahoo. Plaintiff successfully alleged constructive knowledge of infringing activity and materially assisted Yahoo's infringement by virtue of providing photos through licensing agreement when defendant had no basis for believing it had right to use or distribute photos. Motion to dismiss denied.

In re Frontier Communs. Corp., No. 20-22476, slip op. (S.D.N.Y. Bankr. Mar. 27, 2024)

Bankruptcy court declined to dismiss claimants' secondary copyright infringement claims because relevant tests not altered by U.S. Supreme Court decision analyzing secondary criminal liability for aiding and abetting terrorism. Internet service provider Frontier Communications filed voluntary Chapter 11 bankruptcy petition. Various movie and record companies ("Claimants") filed proofs of claims for copyright infringement, alleging contributory and vicarious infringement of their copyrighted works by Frontier subscribers, for which Frontier had received hundreds of thousands of copyright infringement notices. Frontier moved for judgment on pleadings, arguing that, following U.S. Supreme Court's decision in *Twitter v. Taamneh*, internet service providers cannot be held secondarily liable for wrongdoing even if they know specific customers are using their services to do it. In *Twitter*, Supreme Court held that ISP defendants were not liable for aiding and abetting terrorism simply because terrorists were active on their platforms. Court held that, although contributory copyright infringement liability also based on common law aiding-and-abetting principles, because Claimants sufficiently alleged that Frontier knowingly turned blind eye to specific instances of infringement, that infringement not attenuated but occurred on Frontier's platform (as opposed to terrorist attacks at issue in *Twitter*), and that Frontier did more than merely provide its services. Further, court held that *Twitter* did not address or alter vicarious copyright infringement liability, which is rooted in *respondeat superior* theory.

Tremblay v. OpenAI, Inc., Nos. 23-3223, 23-3416, 2024 U.S. Dist. LEXIS 24618 (N.D. Cal. Feb. 12, 2024)

District court dismissed plaintiffs' vicarious copyright infringement claim. Plaintiffs, authors of books who alleges that their books were used to train OpenAI language models operating ChatGPT, sued defendant OpenAI, creator and seller of large language model AI software. Plaintiffs alleged direct and vicarious infringement and DMCA claims. OpenAI copied plaintiffs' copyrighted books and used them in its training dataset. When prompted to summarize books written by each plaintiff, ChatGPT generated accurate summaries. Plaintiffs sought to represent class of all people in U.S. who owned copyright in any work that was used in training data for OpenAI language models. OpenAI moved to dismiss certain claims, including vicarious infringement claim. Defendant argued vicarious infringement claim failed for three reasons: (1) plaintiffs had not alleged direct infringement occurred; (2) plaintiffs did not allege defendants had "right and ability to supervise"; and (3) plaintiffs failed to allege "direct financial interest." Court only considered first argument. Issue was whether plaintiffs showed defendant copied works, demonstrating copying either through direct evidence or by showing defendant had access to plaintiff's work and two works shared similarities probative of copying. As part of second required prong in showing direct infringement, unlawful appropriation, court noted hallmark is that works share substantial similarities. Plaintiffs argued they did not need to allege "substantial similarity" because they had evidence of direct copying: defendant directly copied copyrighted books to train language models. Here, however, plaintiffs failed to allege that ChatGPT outputs contained direct copies of copyrighted books. Because they failed to allege direct copying, they had to show substantial similarity between outputs and copyrighted material. Plaintiffs' complaint failed to allege any particular ChatGPT output was substantially similar, or similar at all, to their books, so court dismissed vicarious copyright infringement claim.

DISH Network LLC v. Jadoo TV, Inc., No. 20-1891, 2023 U.S. Dist. LEXIS 102984 (N.D. Cal. June 13, 2023)

Court granted plaintiff's motion for summary judgment where defendant found to have contributorily and vicariously infringed plaintiff's copyrighted television channels and exclusively licensed content by providing access to users via set-top boxes ("STBs") and mobile applications, advertising and profiting from such infringement, and failing to stop it despite having means to do so. Plaintiff content and television channel provider sued defendant company and its CEO for making its protected channels (that included registered and not registered but otherwise protected works) available to defendants' users through preconfigured STBs it sold to its customers. Content on defendants' devices was largely from publicly available links (e.g., YouTube), but through eMedia service, users could—and did—upload all of plaintiff's registered and unregistered works in South Asian Super Pack ("SASP"—collection of channels, including plaintiff's protected channels). Defendants programmed later STB models to automatically locate and preconfigure SASP even after receiving notices of infringement from plaintiff alleging it had exclusive right to perform protected channels. Defendants only blocked or removed access of protected channels—and ultimately removed section of STB with user-uploaded content, thereby ending infringement—after plaintiff filed present action in November 2018. Plaintiff argued defendants committed contributory infringement by materially contributing to and inducing infringement. Court agreed, finding (1) defendants had actual knowledge that specific infringing material was available using their system, and (2) they could have taken simple measures to prevent further infringement. Defendants were on notice about infringement after receiving plaintiff's letter in August 2016 but continued to perform works until August 2019. They could have taken simple measures, e.g., not installing eMedia player that allowed SASP, but did not. Court agreed with plaintiff's separate theory for contributory infringement based on inducement. Defendants argued their object was promoting product or service to infringe copyrighted work, but court noted defendants advertised eMedia tool for users to upload and watch content not licensed by defendants. Court separately analyzed plaintiff's vicarious infringement claim, finding defendants profited from infringement where it attracted additional users to buy STBs and use service, generating millions. Second, defendants had legal right to stop or limit directly infringing content and practical ability to do so. Indeed, defendants did eventually stop infringement by removing eMedia.

In Lux Rsch. v. Hull McGuire PC, No. 23-523, 2023 U.S. Dist. LEXIS 166700 (D.D.C. Sept. 19, 2023)

District court dismissed plaintiffs' secondary infringement claim against moving defendants—individuals and law firms who represented Proud Boys during 2022 *Nordean* insurrection trial—where plaintiffs failed to adequately allege moving defendants substantially participated in any alleged infringement proven. To support motion to transfer venue out of Washington, D.C. during Proud Boys trial in 2022, plaintiffs—jury polling company and owner—were hired to conduct study on community attitudes toward January 6 defendants. Plaintiffs interacted primarily with non-moving defendant Hull, completing study and report at Hull's urging but without receiving any of agreed-on $30,000 fee. Defendant Hull represented backing from moving defendants on multiple occasions and submitted plaintiffs' report as attachment to motion to supplement motion to transfer venue, stating it was submitted on behalf of all five defendants. One set of moving defendants filed motion for plaintiff owner to testify in support of motion to transfer venue. After submitting report, plaintiffs asked defendants about payment and received no response. Plaintiffs filed cease-and-desist letter, demanding defendants take down and cease all uses of report. Shortly after, plaintiffs registered report with U.S. Copyright Office and sent additional takedown notice demanding payment based on copyright infringement. Hearing nothing, plaintiffs filed complaint—and later amended complaint—against eight defense lawyers and five law firms involved in *Nordean* case. All defendants other than Hull defendants moved to dismiss plaintiffs' secondary copyright infringement claim that covered both contributory and vicarious infringement. Court outlined requirements to make out claim of contributory infringement—(1) direct infringement by third party; (2) knowledge by defendant that third parties were directly infringing; and (3) substantial participation by defendant in infringing activities—and noted that even assuming plaintiffs plausibly alleged direct infringement by Hull defendants and knowledge by moving defendants, they had not adequately alleged moving defendants substantially participated in infringement. Public records showed moving defendants did not "join" only *Nordean* filing that actually used plaintiffs' report, as plaintiffs argued. Court turned to vicarious liability argument, requiring "right and ability" to supervise infringing activity and direct financial interest in such activities. Court found it far from clear plaintiffs plausibly alleged moving defendants had financial interest in unauthorized reproduction and distribution of report and noted that Amended Complaint was devoid of any facts showing moving defendants had right or ability (let alone both) to supervise infringing activity. Plaintiffs offered only conclusory statement that defendants were secondarily liable. Nowhere did plaintiffs allege agreement for Hull defendants to act on behalf of all criminal defendants or that Hull was employee, contractor, or agent of moving defendants. Therefore, court dismissed claim as to moving defendants.

Concord Music Grp., Inc. v. X Corp., No. 23-606, 2024 U.S. Dist. LEXIS 38239 (M.D. Tenn. Mar. 5, 2024)

District court granted defendant's motion to dismiss claims of direct and vicarious infringement, and granted in part and denied in part defendant's motion to dismiss claim of contributory infringement. Plaintiffs, music publishers, alleged defendant X (formerly known as Twitter) directly, contributorily and vicariously infringed plaintiffs' music composition copyrights by allowing and even encouraging users of X platform to post content incorporating unauthorized usage of works and failing to remove infringing posts. Defendant did not dispute occurrences of copyright infringement by users on X platform, but argued plaintiff's claims failed to sufficiently allege defendant (1) engaged in any affirmative conduct constituting unauthorized copying or transmission of works so as to commit direct infringement; (2) "induced or intended to foster the alleged infringement by its users" so as to commit contributory infringement; or (3) had "practical ability to supervise the alleged infringement" and reaped financial benefit from infringement, so as to commit vicarious infringement. In assessing direct infringement claim, court found defendant did not "transmit" works under Transmit Clause of Copyright Act, as works were transmitted by defendant's users, and defendant was merely platform via which content was transmitted, analogous to owner of telegraph lines or machines via which users transmitted messages. Accordingly, court granted defendant's motion to dismiss as to direct infringement. As to vicarious infringement, court found no relationship of "actual right of control," akin to agency relationship between employer and employee, between X and users because X had no power to exert editorial control over users' content before such content was posted "other than making the yes-or-no decision of whether … to remove a tweet after it was posted and brought to [defendant's] attention." Accordingly, court granted defendant's motion to dismiss claim of vicarious infringement. As for of contributory infringement claim, court rejected plaintiff's "broad theory that [defendant] is liable for all of the infringement done on its platform because it has, in effect, created a straightforward, intentional infringement facilitation device," as "[m]any of the supposedly problematic practices … are unremarkable features of X/Twitter generally that [defendant] has simply failed to fence off completely from infringers," citing as examples plaintiff's claims of promotional material appearing near infringing posts and users' ability to easily upload infringing content since such features do not make it "easier to post an infringing file than a non-infringing one." However, court denied defendant's motion to dismiss claim of contributory infringement as to certain of plaintiff's claims, which plausibly alleged contributory infringement: (1) defendant's practice of "allow[ing] users to pay for more forgiving treatment under its anti-infringement policies through its 'verified user' program"; (2) defendant's unreasonable delays in responding to notices of infringement; and (3) failing to remove accounts of "severe repeat infringers."

Thomson Reuters Enter. Ctr. GmbH v. Ross Intel. Inc., No. 20-613, 2023 U.S. Dist. LEXIS 170155 (D. Del. Sept. 25, 2023)

District court denied parties' cross-motions for summary judgment. Plaintiff alleged defendant's AI software copied content from plaintiff's Westlaw legal research platform, as defendant's legal research contractor copied written content from Westlaw headnotes to be used as training data for defendant's AI software. Defendant's own expert admitted actual copying of at least 2,830 data sets. Plaintiff moved for summary judgment on infringement claim. Court stated that plaintiff's theory of contributory liability must be substantiated by factual evidence showing defendant had knowledge of, and materially contributed to or induced, contractor's infringement, and plaintiff's theory of vicarious liability must be based on factual evidence showing defendant had right and ability to supervise or control contractor's infringing activity and direct financial interest in such activity, all of which were disputed by parties. Parties' motions for summary judgment denied.

Okolita v. Amazon.com, Inc., No. 22-284, 2023 U.S. Dist. LEXIS 130477 (D. Me. July 28, 2023)

Plaintiff artist and creator of bird costumes for children sued various online marketplaces including eBay alleging platforms sold "counterfeit copies of her costumes," which were advertised using copies of photographs plaintiff created showing her own children wearing costumes. Defendant eBay filed motion to dismiss direct, contributory and vicarious liability claims, arguing that it responded to plaintiff's takedown requests for content infringing her copyright. District court swiftly dismissed direct infringement claims, finding complaint "long on accusation but devoid of facts" showing direct liability on eBay for posting of her copyrighted photos by eBay users. On contributory infringement claims, court considered whether eBay was both in position to control infringing conduct, and whether it authorized such conduct. Court found that eBay did nothing to promote, induce or encourage infringement by eBay users, and that in fact eBay's conduct was "characterized by reaction to the infringing acts of third parties, not preauthorization of those acts." On vicarious liability claim, court considered whether eBay held right and ability to supervise and control infringing activity conducted on its marketplace, and also whether eBay profited from such infringing conduct while declining to exercise right to stop or limit it. Court declined to dismiss vicarious infringement claim, finding such claim plausible, and that determination of claim required "examination of the quality of eBay response to [plaintiff's] takedown requests" not suited for motion to dismiss. Motion to dismiss direct and contributory infringement claims granted and motion to dismiss vicarious infringement claim denied.

D. Miscellaneous

Lane Coder Photography, LLC v. Hearst Corp., No. 22-5071, 2023 U.S. Dist. LEXIS 159200 (S.D.N.Y. Sept. 8, 2023)

District court denied defendants' motion to dismiss plaintiff professional photographer's direct infringement claim. Plaintiff was commissioned by Sotheby's to photograph Connecticut real estate "Greenacre." Pursuant to parties' agreement, Sotheby was to use photos for advertising property's sale and could not sub-license photos or transmit to other parties. Plaintiff obtained group copyright registration of photos. Shortly after, defendant Hearst Corporation published two online articles using several of plaintiff's photos without plaintiff's authorization—some with attribution to Sotheby's, some without. Defendant Yahoo published online article using at least one of plaintiff's photos with no attribution and informed plaintiff it received photos and content for article from defendant Hearst through content license agreement. Plaintiff did not authorize display or use of photos in articles and alleged defendant Hearst obtained photos from Sotheby's website and removed plaintiff's CMI. Defendants move to dismiss direct infringement claim. Court concluded that plaintiff plausibly stated claim for direct infringement. Plaintiff obtained copyright registration for photographs. Further, complaint indicated defendants infringed plaintiff's copyright by reproducing and publicly displaying unauthorized copies of plaintiff's photos in three infringing articles. Court rejected defendants' argument that plaintiff failed to adequately allege he suffered injury due to infringement because existence of damages suffered is not essential element of claim for infringement, especially at motion to dismiss stage. In any event, plaintiff did adequately allege he suffered injury due to defendants' infringement, so motion to dismiss denied as to direct infringement claim.

Jones v. Atl. Records, No. 22-893, 2023 U.S. Dist. LEXIS 152283 (S.D.N.Y. Aug. 29, 2023)

District court granted defendants' motion to dismiss infringement claim. Plaintiff sued defendants for infringement of song lyrics. Defendants argued plaintiff did not allege defendants had access to song, plaintiff did not allege substantial similarity between lyrics, plaintiff's lyrics unoriginal, and plaintiff did not allege specific facts against individual defendants. Court found plaintiff did not adequately allege access because circumstantial alleged connection between defendant and plaintiff's ex-business partner did not meet threshold, nor did facts alleged suggest song was widely disseminated. Court found short phrases over which plaintiff sought copyright protection not protectable because phrases were common and employed frequently in popular culture and other hip-hop songs. Court also found lyrics at issue not substantially similar because phrases used in different ways and had different meanings. Court found dismissal of claims warranted because plaintiff's lyrics not protectable as matter of law and not substantially similar to defendant's lyrics.

Kadrey v. Meta Platforms, Inc., No. 23-3417, 2023 U.S. Dist. LEXIS 207683 (N.D. Cal. Nov. 20, 2023)

District court granted Meta's motion to dismiss several claims regarding use of plaintiffs' books to train its language model. Plaintiff authors brought claims against Meta regarding its LLaMA AI language model, arguing that Meta improperly extracted content of plaintiffs' books to train model. Court found that language models themselves could not possibly be derivative works, as they cannot be understood to be recasting or adaptation of any of plaintiffs' books. Claim that each output of LLaMA produced in response to user query is infringing derivative work for which Meta is vicariously liable failed for lack of allegations of specific contents of any one output, let alone infringing output. Court rejected plaintiffs' arguments that actual copying of books in full spares need to prove similarity between books and output. Court further dismissed DMCA claim because plaintiffs did not allege that Meta distributed plaintiffs' books. Meta did not move to dismiss claim for unauthorized copying of books for purpose of training language model.

DISH Network LLC v. Jadoo TV, Inc., No. 20-1891, 2023 U.S. Dist. LEXIS 102984 (N.D. Cal. June 13, 2023)

Court granted plaintiff's motion for summary judgment where defendant found to have directly infringed plaintiff's copyrighted television channels and exclusively licensed content by providing access to users via set-top boxes ("STBs") and mobile applications. Plaintiff content and television channel provider sued defendant company and its CEO for making its protected channels (that included registered and unregistered but otherwise protected works) available to defendants' users through preconfigured STBs it sold to its customers. Content on defendants' devices was largely from publicly available links (e.g., YouTube), but through eMedia service, users could—and did—upload all of plaintiff's registered and unregistered works in South Asian Super Pack ("SASP"—collection of channels, including plaintiff's protected channels). Defendants programmed later STB models to automatically locate and preconfigure SASP even after receiving notices of infringement from plaintiff alleging it had exclusive right to perform protected channels. Defendants only blocked or removed access of protected channels—and ultimately removed section of STB with user-uploaded content, thereby ending infringement—after plaintiff filed present action in November 2018. Court found direct infringement where it was undisputed plaintiff owned allegedly infringed material. Further, defendants violated plaintiff's exclusive public performance right to by enhancing users' access to infringing content and uploading and instigating content's distribution. Defendants preloaded STBs with content, including eMedia app that allowed user uploads. It preconfigured STBs to automatically locate and install infringing content SASP. Defendants knew of infringement but took no actions to limit it despite having knowledge of infringement and CEO's having ability to remove channels from service. Defendants separately violated plaintiff's exclusive right to perform works because one of defendants' employees—as its agent—uploaded and streamed infringing content. Court found defendants had required volition by selecting material for upload. It also found CEO was personally liable as director because he was "guiding spirit" behind infringement.

Russell v. Walmart Inc., No. 19-5495, 2023 U.S. Dist. LEXIS 151712 (C.D. Cal. Aug. 17, 2023)

District court denied defendant Walmart's renewed motion for judgment as matter of law where there was sufficient evidence for jury to find plaintiff artist and photographer proved copyright infringement on at least one of three alternative theories. Plaintiff argued Walmart infringed her copyrighted photographs by storing them on its servers and displaying copies on its website through publishing product listing that offered to sell sculptures in photographs. Plaintiff also argued Walmart infringed her copyrighted sculptures by selling inferior replicas. Walmart disputed that it published (or caused to be published) photographs in connection with product listings or that it sold any replica products, but contended that third-party retailer displayed photos and sold replica products. After jury verdict in plaintiff's favor on copyright infringement and against defendant on DMCA defense and court entered judgment, defendant filed Rule 50(b) motion. Defendant argued plaintiff failed to prove causation necessary for direct infringement. Court disagreed, noting Walmart's argument essentially asked court to disregard all evidence that supported plaintiff's theory of case. There was sufficient evidence for jury to conclude defendant "caused" copyright infringement of photographs and sculptures. Crucially, defendant was actively involved in infringement beyond mere operation of its website: product listings stated replicas "sold and shipped by Walmart"; defendant's category specialists or managers had to approve companies before they could sell on Walmart.com as Direct Ship Vendors ("DSVs"); before product could be offered or sold on defendant's website, DSVs had to provide product images and descriptions; photographs associated with product listings were stored on defendant's servers; and Walmart's category specialists had final say regarding content appearing on Walmart.com. Evidence sufficient for jury to find causation or volitional conduct for infringement. Similarly, sufficient evidence regarding sculptures where defendant took title over infringing replicas and itself designated shipping arrangements to deliver them to customers.

InfoGroup Inc. v. Office Depot, Inc., No. 23-80358, 2023 U.S. Dist. LEXIS 106276 (S.D. Fla. June 20, 2023)

District court granted defendant's motion to dismiss complaint alleging infringement of plaintiff's copyrighted databases, finding that databases were within scope of license agreement in place between parties. Plaintiff licensed databases consisting of "demographic, marketing and other related information" on millions of businesses ("Works") to defendant to "use the [Works] for its own direct marketing and internal research and analytics." Agreement was entered into on behalf of defendant by representative from defendant's marketing department. Plaintiff alleged infringement occurred when defendant provided Works to defendant's real estate department for purposes of making real estate decisions, such as choosing retail store locations, arguing agreement only permitted use of Works by defendant's marketing department and for direct marketing purposes. Plaintiff argued in support of claims that Agreement was entered into on behalf of defendant by representative from defendant's marketing department and that limitation of license of Works to use by marketing department was established by "other provisions" and language in Agreement referring to license as "DM License" and "direct marketing license." Court agreed with defendant that plain language of agreement did not restrict usage of Works to exclude internal real estate-related purposes, as agreement was entered into by defendant with no limitation to marketing department. Court also rejected plaintiff's argument that use of terms "DM license" and "direct marketing license" in agreement, was sufficient to limit defendant's use of Works to marketing department only.

Stokes v. Brinor, Inc., No. 22-973, 2023 U.S. Dist. LEXIS 123840 (N.D. Oh. July 18, 2023)

District court granted summary judgment for plaintiff on liability. Plaintiff accused defendant saloon of displaying flyer on its Facebook page containing altered version of plaintiff's photograph. Plaintiff sued for infringement and moved for summary judgment on liability. Defendant argued that flyer designer was responsible for creating infringing flyer, and court agreed, but court found that defendant still violated plaintiff's right to reproduce underlying photograph when it posted flyer to Facebook. Defendant's lack of knowledge that photo was copyrighted was no defense to infringement. Court granted summary judgment on liability.

VI. DEFENSES/EXEMPTIONS

A. Fair Use

Am. Soc'y for Testing & Materials v. Pub. Resource.Org, Inc., 82 F.4th 1262 (D.C. Cir. 2023)

Plaintiffs National Fire Protection Association, American Society for Testing and Materials, and American Society of Heating, Refrigerating, and Air Conditioning Engineers all developed and sold hard copy industry standards. Defendant Public.Resource.Org is non-profit organization that published plaintiffs' copyrighted standards online. Plaintiffs previously moved for summary judgment on certain standards, which district court granted, and it rejected defendant's argument that posting standards incorporated by reference into law constituted fair use. D.C. Circuit reversed and remanded for district court to consider fair use defense. On remand, parties submitted further information about 217 standards at issue, and district court found that posting 184 of standards—those incorporated by reference into law—constituted fair use, 32 of standards—those not incorporated by reference into law—did not constitute fair use, and posting one standard constituted fair use in part. District court did not award injunctive relief because defendant indicated that it only intended to publish standards incorporated by reference into law and would take down those that were not incorporated into law in response to decision. Plaintiff appealed. D.C. Circuit affirmed, finding that fair use insulated defendant from infringement as to those standards incorporated into reference by law. On first factor, court highlighted fact that defendant was not engaged in commercial use; it also found that defendant's use was transformative, relying in part on Supreme Court's *Warhol v. Goldsmith* decision, finding that plaintiffs and defendant had different purposes in publishing standards. Plaintiffs seek to advance their industry by publishing best practices, while defendant "publishes only what the law is." Court found second factor to strongly counsel in favor of fair use since standards were closer to fact-based material. On third fair factor, court highlighted fact that it was reasonable for defendant to post entire standard if entire standard had been incorporated by reference into law. On fourth factor, court was not persuaded by plaintiffs' argument regarding market harm—that if users can download standards for free, no one would buy their print industry guides. There may still be market for up-to-date guides, even when law has not yet incorporated by reference those new standards. Court also balanced plaintiffs' potential loss against "public benefit" defendant provided in posting standards. Circuit Court also found that district court did not abuse its discretion in failing to award injunction, given that defendant quickly removed 32 standards that district court found to infringe.

Whyte Monkee Prods., LLC v. Netflix, Inc., 97 F.4th 699 (10th Cir. 2024)

Court reversed and remanded district court on issue of fair use where it disagreed with district court's ruling on first and fourth factors. Defendants Netflix and Royal Goode Productions released seven-part documentary *Tiger King: Murder, Mayhem and Madness* in March 2020. *Tiger King* featured clips from eight videos filmed by videographer plaintiff—seven while he was working for Gerald Wayne Interactive Zoological Park ("Park") and one after plaintiff terminated his relationship with Park. Following release of *Tiger King*, plaintiffs registered eight videos and sued defendants for copyright infringement, claiming plaintiffs owned copyrights in videos and defendants used clips without permission. Video at issue, "Travis MM Funeral Ceremony" was approximately 24 minutes long and documented funeral of Park founder Joe Exotic's husband. Clip appears in segment of *Tiger King* lasting about one minute and six seconds, focusing on portions of Mr. Exotic's eulogy. Defendants argued their use of eighth video qualified as fair use and that no copyright infringement had occurred. Tenth Circuit held that district court erred in determining defendants were entitled to summary judgment on their fair use defense, erroneously concluding first and fourth factors weighed in defendants' favor. On first factor, purpose and character of use, court disagreed with district court's finding that defendants' use of clip was transformative. Citing *Warhol v. Goldsmith*, court agreed with plaintiffs that streaming use was "as commercial as it gets" and was not transformative because it made no commentary on work itself. Instead, defendants used video to comment on Joe Exotic, highlighting his megalomania. On second factor, court agreed with district court's finding factor weighed in favor of defendants because funeral video was "indisputably factual, containing only footage of only actual events." Further, plaintiffs livestreamed funeral video to YouTube, allowing public to copy. On third factor, amount and substantiality of material used, court agreed with district court that factor favored defendants. As threshold matter, defendants used one minute of video lasting 24 minutes—only about five percent. Defendants used no more of video than necessary, and what they did use was reasonable in light of "providing historical reference points of Mr. Exotic's life." Court held that district court incorrectly analyzed fourth factor because it failed to cite to any evidence in record demonstrating absence of market impact. Because district court erroneously concluded fourth factor weighed in defendants' favor, Court of Appeals could not determine whether defendants' use of funeral video was fair use. Court reversed and remanded.

Philpot v. Indep. J. Review, 92 F.4th 252 (4th Cir. 2024)

Fourth Circuit reversed district court's grant of summary judgment for defendant based on fair use. Plaintiff, photographer Larry Philpot, alleged that defendant Independent Journal Review ("IJR") infringed his photograph of musician Ted Nugent in online article. Defendant moved for summary judgment on fair use defense. District court granted summary judgment to IJR on fair use. Regarding fair use, Fourth Circuit evaluated first factor in light of Supreme Court's *Warhol v. Goldsmith* holding, noting that defendant's use of subject work was not transformative, because plaintiff took photo as portrait of Nugent, while IJR used photo to depict Nugent—in other words, both used photo for substantially same purpose, with nearly minimal alterations to photo by IJR, and without adding new meaning or function that would establish transformative use. In addition, court concluded that defendant used photo for commercial purpose, because it derived (minimal) advertising revenue from article containing photo and did not pay customary price for use of photo. Regarding second and third factors—not discussed by district court—Fourth Circuit held that both weighed against fair use: photograph was highly creative, and IJR copied significant portion of photo. Regarding fourth factor, IJR claimed that plaintiff allowed free use of subject work, and therefore there was no financial harm to potential market. Fourth Circuit disagreed, noting presumption that market harm exists where commercial use is not transformative and involves mere duplication of subject work.

Furthermore, court held plaintiff's decision not to charge certain users of photo immaterial to effect of defendant's use on potential market, in part because plaintiff's potential market would likely dwindle if defendant's behavior became widespread. Fourth Circuit therefore held that all four factors weighed against fair use.

August Image, LLC v. Girard Ent. & Media LLC, No. 23-1492, 2024 U.S. Dist. LEXIS 59790 (S.D.N.Y. Apr. 1, 2024)

Court granted motion to dismiss on fair use grounds, in case involving unauthorized use of photograph depicting cast of TV series "Friends." Plaintiff created photograph in 1995, and it appeared on cover of Rolling Stone magazine. Cast member David Schwimmer subsequently included photograph in Instagram post ("Post"), together with caption "It's happening". In February 2020, Defendants published article entitled "Can Friends Reboot Count on Aging Fans to Rekindle Love of TV Show?" ("Article"). Article included screenshot of Post, including photograph, and stated that "Schwimmer … confirmed in an Instagram post that the cast had agreed on a 'Friends' special." Defendants moved for judgment on pleadings under Rule 12(c), arguing that Article made fair use of photograph. Court observed in footnote that courts "generally wait until the summary judgment phase to address fair use," but dismissal is warranted where "fair use is clearly established on the face of the complaint." Here, first factor weighed "heavily" for fair use because Article "communicates something new and different from the original [photograph]" and is therefore transformative. (Court failed to mention Supreme Court decision in *Warhol v. Goldsmith*, which questioned similar reasoning.) Inclusion of photograph was "incidental" to "the Article's focus," i.e., possible "Friends" reunion: "That purpose was wholly distinct from the purpose for which the Photograph was taken, which was to depict the cast of Friends." Even though Article "never directly discussed" photograph, Court held that "secondary use need not comment on the Photo *per se*" to be transformative. Second factor weighed "weakly" against fair use because photograph was creative. Third factor was "neutral" because "copying the entirety of a work is sometimes necessary to make a fair use." Court found that "to copy any less would have made the picture useless to the story," but as court had previously determined that photograph was "incidental" to Post, and to Article, this reasoning is somewhat unclear. Fourth factor was also "neutral," but court found that there was no plausible allegation that Article "could, in any way, impair any other market for commercial use of the photo, or diminish its value." (Court did not discuss possible harm to licensing market, which was major focus of *Warhol* decision.) Having found third and fourth factors neutral, and second factor weighing against fair use, court nonetheless found that fair use was "clearly established" and dismissed without leave to amend. Notice of appeal was filed.

Wilder v. Hoiland, No. 22-1254, 2024 U.S. Dist. LEXIS 18051 (S.D.N.Y. Feb. 1, 2024)

District court granted defendant's motion for summary judgment based on fair use defense. Plaintiff Esther Wilder, faculty member at City University of New York, sued another CUNY faculty member, Sarah Hoiland, for alleged infringement of plaintiff's written materials focused on assisting educators in developing assessment plans and instruction for measuring success of infusing numeracy and quantitative reasoning in classrooms ("Unit 7H"). Plaintiff prepared Unit 7H as part of faculty development program entitled NICHE, which was funded by National Science Foundation grant. In February 2019, defendant Hoiland attended conference for community college educators and presented slides containing portions of text of Unit 7H. Defendant did not include plaintiff's name in slides, but claimed to have orally referenced plaintiff numerous times during presentation. Plaintiff obtained copy of defendant's presentation, then registered copyright in Unit 7H materials in April 2021 and subsequently filed suit. First fair use factor weighed in favor of defendant, as district court held that defendant's use of subject work was transformative, because original work was used to teach faculty at CUNY regarding how to infuse and assess quantitative reasoning in their courses, whereas defendant used work at community college conference, primarily in connection with discussing how to recruit and motivate faculty in professional development; in addition, defendant's use of work was for educational, non-commercial purpose. Second factor also weighed in defendant's favor, because Unit 7H text was not work of fiction. Third factor weighed slightly in favor of plaintiff, as defendant had used approximately two-thirds of text in deposit copy, though court noted that defendant had removed many essential portions of plaintiff's work. Regarding fourth factor, district court concluded that potential market for Unit 7H text would be limited and had little commercial or professional value without broader written work within which Unit 7H resided. In addition, transformative use of work by defendant reduced potential for economic harm to plaintiff. In light of these considerations, court held that defendant successfully established fair use defense as matter of law.

Stebbins v. Google LLC, No. 23-322, 2023 U.S. Dist. LEXIS 169937 (N.D. Cal. Aug. 31, 2023)

District court granted defendant Google's motion to dismiss plaintiff's claim for copyright infringement. Plaintiff was YouTuber and Twitch streamer who went by name "Acerthorn." Another YouTube user set up YouTube channel titled "Acerthorn the True Acerthorn" to harass, doxx, and impersonate plaintiff and infringe his copyright. Plaintiff alleged that frame of plaintiff's livestream had been used as icon for "Acerthorn the True Acerthorn," and brought suit against Google for copyright infringement for hosting icon on its servers. Plaintiff moved for summary judgment, asking court to adjudge that Acerthorn the True Acerthorn channel "is not a 'fair use channel' and therefore, that all other elements of the channel are entirely irrelevant to determining whether the icon is fair use," failing to cite to legal authority. Google moved to dismiss infringement claim, arguing Acerthorn the True Acerthorn channel's use of icon was fair use because "(1) the allegedly-infringing icon is a transformative use of Plaintiff's livestream; (2) the livestream was of minimal creative value; (3) the icon is a small portion of the livestream; and (4) Plaintiff has not alleged any economic impact to the livestream in relation to the icon." Court agreed with defendant, finding all factors weighed in favor of fair use finding. Court denied plaintiff's motion for summary judgment and granted defendant's motion to dismiss.

Chosen Figure LLC v. Kevin Frazier Prods., No. 22-06518, 2023 U.S. Dist. LEXIS 125669 (C.D. Cal. July 19, 2023)

Plaintiff, photographer, captured photograph of recording artists Rihanna and A$AP Rocky standing next to one another ("Photograph"). Another recording artist, Lil Uzi Vert, reproduced Photograph on his Instagram stories, superimposing "Cant Be True" in corner ("Story"). Defendant, owner and operator of Black-focused entertainment news website Hip Hollywood, published article chronicling Lil Uzi Vert's reaction to Rihanna being seen in public with A$AP Rocky and including screenshot of Story. Defendant moved to dismiss plaintiff's copyright infringement claim on fair use grounds, arguing that subject of article was Lil Uzi Vert's Story rather than people in Photograph. Court held that defendant's use not transformative because article was entirely based on Photograph's existence: article's first sentence discussed Rihanna and A$AP Rocky's relationship and Photograph itself (not just Story), and, in any case, Story also concerned persons in Photograph. Moreover, court noted that defendant had hosted "fixed" copy of Photograph on its website, which distinguished situation from another case in which Instagram post had been embedded but was still hosted on Instagram's servers. Defendant's reproduction of entire Photograph, potential impact on plaintiff's licensing market, and arguably artistic nature of Photograph all weighed against fair use finding.

In Lux Rsch. v. Hull McGuire PC, No. 23-523, 2024 U.S. Dist. LEXIS 31848 (D.D.C. Feb. 26, 2024)

Defendant lawyers represented certain Proud Boys in January 6 cases and engaged plaintiff to conduct "jury-polling analysis" in support of motion to transfer cases out of District of Columbia. Plaintiff sued for infringement, alleging defendants never paid for jury reports and that defendants instead copied jury report from separate January 6 case from public docket and submitted it in additional cases without authorization. On motion to dismiss, defendants asserted fair use defense and argued they did nothing more than "moving a 'publicly filed report in Pacer [] from one case location docket [] to another." District court initially noted that fair use "normally calls for an extensive review of the factual record generated by discovery," and as such is rarely reached on motion to dismiss. But even if court were to consider fair use defense on motion to dismiss, district court rejected defendants' argument that its copying of report was "for the purpose of 'educat[ing]… the Court," and thus noncommercial fair use. After criticizing defendants' briefing strategy as "blitz[ing] this Court with so many pages of case citations that, in its exhaustion, it will simply relent and agree with their conclusory statement," court found that defendants never addressed body of caselaw finding that "use of copyrighted material created for the purpose of litigation or arbitration in a separate litigation—i.e., for the same purpose for which the work was created—is not fair use." District court similarly rejected defendants' argument that their use of work was excused under "first-sale doctrine," finding that even if defendants owned copy of plaintiff's work, reproduction of work by posting report to public docket would nevertheless constitute infringement. Moreover, defendants never addressed that they were not even owner of copy of report, given that they never paid plaintiff for report. Motion to dismiss under fair use and first sale doctrines denied.

Cooley v. Marcus, No. 23-86, 2023 U.S. Dist. LEXIS 127119 (W.D. Mich. July 24, 2023)

District court granted in part and denied in part defendant's motion to dismiss complaint. According to complaint, defendant posted video to GoFundMe fundraising page that featured photos and video recordings of Elle Roskamp, defendant's sister, who was missing person. Approximately 17 months later, plaintiff registered copyright in several photos and videos appearing in plaintiff's GoFundMe video. Defendant asserted defense of fair use. Regarding first fair use factor, court held that available facts from complaint did not allow for determination of purpose of use. Regarding second factor, district court noted that it lacked full circumstances surrounding creation of copyrighted works at issue, which affected whether works were creative or factual in nature. Regarding third factor, court held that it lacked sufficient information regarding whether photos and videos appearing in defendant's video were full copies of plaintiffs' copyrighted works, or only partial copies of larger works. Finally, regarding fourth factor, district court held that, based on facts available from complaint, it was unable to assess value of or potential market for plaintiffs' copyrighted works. District court therefore declined to resolve fair use defense, and denied defendant's motion to dismiss complaint based on alleged fair use.

Cramer v. Netflix, Inc., No. 22-131, 2023 U.S. Dist. LEXIS 165510 (W.D. Pa. Sept. 18, 2023)

District court granted defendant's motion to dismiss infringement claim, finding defendant's use of tattoo was fair use. Plaintiff sued defendant for infringement arising from defendant's use of plaintiff's tattoo of Joe Exotic on her husband, which aired in episode of *Tiger King*. Allegedly infringing photo was shown in episode without reference or attribution to plaintiff. Defendant argued use was fair use. Court held purpose and character of use weighed strongly in favor of defendants. Plaintiff's purpose in creating tattoo was to capitalize on Joe Exotic's popularity in order to sell gift certificates. Defendant's purpose for using image of tattoo was to include online postings relating to *Tiger King* to give audience sense of public's reaction to Joe Exotic phenomenon. Court found defendant's use of image of tattoo independent from plaintiff's original purpose, and to neither supersedes object of tattoo nor serve as substitute. Court found nature of copyrighted work creative, but defendant's use transformative. Court held amount and substantiality of portion used favored fair use because image of tattoo was shown in entirety, but less than life-sized and depicted along with seven other images on screen, and shown for less than three seconds. Court found use did not create likelihood of market harm for tattoo or plaintiff's ability to sell gift cards or drive income; effect of use upon potential market for or value of copyrighted work favored fair use. Plaintiff did not show defendant's use had meaningful or significant effect on potential market for or value of tattoo. Court found plaintiff and defendant had wholly unrelated products and different marketing channels, so use did not usurp market for original. Viewing allegations in light most favorable to plaintiff, court held it could not grant relief under any set of facts proven consistent with record, so court entered judgment for defendant.

> *Thiccc Boy Prod. v. Swindelles*, No. 22-90, 2024 U.S. Dist. LEXIS 30287 (D.R.I. Feb. 22, 2024)

Court denied plaintiff's motion for summary judgment and granted defendant's motion for summary judgment, finding defendant's use of plaintiff's copyrighted material was fair. Plaintiff production company and producer of *The Fighter and the Kid* podcast sued defendant YouTube content creator for publishing several videos that included segments of plaintiff's copyrighted work to his YouTube page. Plaintiff's podcast was recorded in both audio and video, and defendant published four videos that were subject of this case in which plaintiff alleged copyright infringement. Plaintiff claimed fair use. Court analyzed fair use factors. On purpose and character of use, court found factor weighed in favor of defendant because his "reaction videos" used copyrighted works to criticize or comment on them rather than supersede works' original objects. On nature of copyrighted works, court found factor again weighed in favor of defendant because copyrighted works were published works that were more factual than creative. Specifically, copyrighted videos essentially consist of three men in recording studio talking about current events in popular culture and their personal lives, akin to talk show. Court found third factor, amount and substantiality of portion used, weighed in favor of plaintiff because defendant copied more material than was necessary; he duplicated copyrighted videos' full frames, and all videos contained segments of copyrighted videos that defendant did not criticize or comment on. Finally, factor regarding effect of use upon potential market for copyrighted work weighed in favor of defendant because his videos functioned as criticism or commentary and were unlikely to function as substitutes for copyrighted videos in their original and potential derivative markets. In weighing all factors, court concluded that defendant's use of copyrighted material was fair.

Facility Guidelines Inst., Inc. v. Upcodes, Inc., 677 F. Supp. 3d 955 (E.D. Mo. 2023)

Court denied plaintiff Facility Guidelines Institute, Inc.'s ("FGI") motion for preliminary injunction. FGI published guidelines relating to construction of healthcare facilities. Defendant Upcodes, Inc. ("Upcodes") published FGI's guidelines that have been adopted into law by certain jurisdictions. Court held that FGI did not carry its burden in showing that it was likely to succeed on merits of infringement claim due to fair use defense. On first factor, court found defendant's use, posting laws to educate members of the public, was transformative and defendant had significant justification for copying. Court similarly found second and third factor to weigh in favor of fair use—guidelines were factual, and defendant copied only what had been enacted into law. On fourth factor, effect of Upcodes's use on market for FGI's work, court found that FGI did not establish extent of market impact. Court denied motion for preliminary injunction.

Thomson Reuters Enter. Ctr. GmbH v. Ross Intel. Inc., No. 20-613, 2023 U.S. Dist. LEXIS 170155 (D. Del. Sept. 25, 2023)

District court denied parties' cross-motions for summary judgment. Plaintiff alleged defendant's AI software copied content from plaintiff's Westlaw legal research platform, as defendant's legal research contractor copied written content from Westlaw headnotes to be used as training data for defendant's AI software. Defendant's own expert admitted actual copying of at least 2,830 data sets. Both parties moved for summary judgment on defendant's fair use defense. Regarding defendant's fair use arguments, court found jury must determine whether use is transformative where defendant's software studied works to "analyze language patterns, not to replicate Westlaw's expression" and extent to which defendant's AI outputs were substantially similar to works. Parties' motions for summary judgment on fair use denied.

Campbell v. Gannett Co., No. 21-557, 2023 U.S. Dist. LEXIS 142188 (W.D. Mo. Aug. 15, 2023)

District court denied defendants' summary judgment motion based on fair use. Plaintiff sued defendants for direct, contributory, and vicarious infringement and removal of copyright management information in connection with plaintiff's photograph of National Football League Coach Katie Sowers. Pursuant to license agreement, photo of Sowers was used in Microsoft ad entitled "Be The One" that aired during Super Bowl Commercial in 2020. Screenshot of plaintiff's photo was displayed on websites owned by defendants in connection with "Ad Meter" public survey regarding Super Bowl commercials. Defendants asserted fair use defense. Regarding first factor, court held that factfinder could reasonably find that defendants used subject work for commercial purpose, and was not transformative; true purpose of making Super Bowl ads—including subject work—available for commentary was to generate more revenue for defendants' Ad Meter service. Regarding second factor, factfinder could reasonably find that subject work was primarily creative, in part because it expressed historic moment of Coach Sowers as first openly gay and female coach in NFL to reach Super Bowl. Regarding third factor, defendants used plaintiff's entire photo in high resolution, which weighed against fair use. Regarding fourth factor, court found triable issue of fact, because defendants argued that in many instances subject work was altered to include play button when used in connection with Ad Meter service and was therefore not market substitute. Considering all four factors in total, district court held that defendants failed to meet their burden of showing they were entitled to judgment as matter of law on their fair use affirmative defense.

Dermansky v. Hayride Media, LLC, No. 22-3491, 2023 U.S. Dist. LEXIS 168076 (E.D. La. Sept. 21, 2023)

District court granted plaintiff's motion for partial summary judgment and denied defendant's motion for summary judgment, holding that fair use defense failed as matter of law. Plaintiff Julie Dermansky, professional photographer, alleged that defendant Hayride, which operated conservative news blog and website, used plaintiff's photos of St. Tammany, Louisiana councilman speaking to anti-fracking protestors and of Baton Rouge community activist standing in front of flood-damaged belongings without approval, without paying licensing fee, and without crediting plaintiff. Defendant sought dismissal of infringement claims based on fair use defense. Regarding first fair use factor, defendant derived direct commercial benefit from use of subject works, and use was not transformative. Referencing Supreme Court's recent *Warhol v. Goldsmith* decision, district court noted that use was not transformative because both plaintiff and defendants used photos as illustrative images for online news articles. Factual dispute regarding whether defendant lacked good faith in its use of images of photos was immaterial, because defendant failed to prove transformative use. Regarding second factor, plaintiff made "deliberate and intentional creative choices" that made works creative in nature, not just informational. Regarding third factor, defendant used substantial portion of works, because its purpose in using works was similar to plaintiff's, i.e., to illustrate news articles. Regarding fourth factor, defendant's use of plaintiff's works was deemed to be market substitute for original works, even though plaintiff and defendant had opposing political viewpoints. All four factors therefore weighed against fair use. Court accordingly denied defendant's motion for summary judgment and granted plaintiff's cross-motion.

B. Statute of Limitations

Wanjuan Media (Tianjin) Co., Ltd. v. Amazon.Com, Inc., No. 22-1434, 2024 U.S. Dist. LEXIS 41209 (S.D.N.Y. Mar. 8, 2024)

Plaintiff television production and distribution company based in Tianjin, China alleged ownership of Chinese language historical drama television show *General and I*, and sued Amazon for infringement for streaming work via Amazon Prime. On cross motions for summary judgment, district court considered defendant Amazon's argument that claim was untimely as filed more than three years after work was removed from streaming platform, and plaintiff's counter-argument that although Act may limit damages to three years prior to filing of suit, Second Circuit precedent permits claims to be brought up to three years following discovery of infringement. Finding that work was available for streaming on Amazon through October 2018, but that plaintiff learned of alleged infringement in in September 2021 and filed suit in February 2022, district court considered whether claim was brought within three-year statute of limitations under Act. District court noted Second Circuit precedent (most recently reaffirmed in *Sohm v. Scholastic*) clearly embraces "discovery rule" under which claim does not accrue "until the copyright holder discovers, or with due diligence should have discovered" infringement. Despite Amazon's arguments and citations to courts outside of Second Circuit rejecting discovery rule, district court found claim was timely brought under discovery rule, within three years of plaintiff's learning of alleged infringement. Defendant Amazon's motion for summary judgment on statute of limitations denied.

McGlynn v. Sinovision Inc., No. 23-4826, 2024 U.S. Dist. LEXIS 26641 (S.D.N.Y. Feb. 15, 2024)

Plaintiff, photographer, took photo of Hamilton Fish Park Pool in 2015 and registered copyright in photo in 2017. In 2022, plaintiff observed its photo displayed on defendant's website in article dated July 2017 and, in 2023, filed suit. Defendant moved to dismiss, arguing that plaintiff's suit should be time barred because plaintiff was sophisticated serial copyright infringement litigant who should have, with reasonable diligence, discovered infringing photograph prior to 2022. Court denied motion, finding that record of past lawsuits was insufficient, on its own, to charge plaintiff with constructive discovery of alleged infringement prior to 2022.

Jackson v. Destiny's Child, No. 23-10507, 2024 U.S. Dist. LEXIS 13019 (S.D.N.Y. Jan. 18, 2024)

District court dismissed plaintiff's claims that accrued more than three years prior to complaint filing date. *Pro se* plaintiff wrote song called "Assumptions Day" in 1996 and registered it in 2001. Between 1997 through early 2000s, plaintiff was hospitalized in mental hospital claiming that he had mental anguish due to discovery that his song was infringed by several artists. On November 30, 2023, plaintiff filed suit against Destiny's Child, claiming that their song "Say My Name" infringed his copyright. Despite alleging that "Say My Name" was released in 1999, plaintiff claimed he did not become aware of infringement until 2023. Court held that, due to Copyright Act's three-year statute of limitations, plaintiff's claims were untimely as to any claims accruing prior to November 30, 2020. That plaintiff had been in mental hospital was insufficient to be extraordinary circumstance that would have rendered plaintiff unable to discover infringement earlier and pursue copyright infringement claims earlier. However, due to plaintiff's *pro se* status, court granted leave to replead and allege facts showing why earlier claims were timely or why statute of limitations should be equitably tolled.

Bridgeport Music, Inc. v. TufAmerica, Inc., No. 19-1764, 2023 U.S. Dist. LEXIS 159845 (S.D.N.Y. Sep. 10, 2023)

District court denied defendant's motion to reconsider prior grant of summary judgment dismissing infringement counterclaim as time barred, when predecessor to defendant became aware of claim in 1970s and defendant was on inquiry notice as soon as it purchased predecessor's rights in 2011. Label for which funk musician George Clinton recorded compositions in 1960s went bankrupt in that decade. Clinton then began recording music for plaintiff, and in 1970s re-recorded compositions that had originally been recorded for bankrupt label. Plaintiffs registered those compositions with Copyright Office between 1970s and 1990s. In 2011, defendant purchased purported ownership interest in compositions from widow of owner of bankrupt label. In 2017, defendant sent letter to plaintiffs claiming to own compositions and accusing plaintiffs of infringement. Plaintiffs filed complaint for declaratory judgment that they owned compositions, and defendants counterclaimed for infringement. Court granted summary judgment dismissing defendant's claim as time barred, finding that it accrued in 1970s when plaintiff re-recorded and registered compositions, at which time owner of bankrupt label played these re-recorded versions in his capacity as radio disc jockey without receiving royalties. Defendant was then on inquiry notice of claim upon purchasing purported rights from widow in 2011. Defendant then moved for reconsideration, arguing that whether bankrupt label owner played re-recorded versions on radio was disputed fact in Rule 56.1 Statement, which court ignored. Court denied motion for reconsideration, noting that defendant failed to argue in summary judgment briefing that this fact was disputed, and party cannot raise new argument on motion to reconsider. Court further found that fact was properly supported by record, and there was no evidentiary basis for defendant to dispute it.

Moss v. Miller, No. 23-7424, 2023 U.S. Dist. LEXIS 226013 (C.D. Cal. Dec. 15, 2023)

District court dismissed declaratory relief claim brought by two of decedent's children. Songwriter Ron Miller died in 2007. At that time his estranged wife Aurora Miller became entitled to 50% interest, and each of Ron's four children became entitled to 12.5% interest, in Ron's termination interests with respect to copyrights in songs he had written. Complaint alleged that one child, Lisa, improperly influenced Aurora for purpose of using their combined majority interest in copyright termination interests to execute numerous notices of termination from August 2009 through April 2016, with several allegedly executed after Aurora lacked capacity to understand, consent to, or execute legal documents, and two allegedly executed after Aurora was in coma and "essentially brain dead." In 2018 Lisa's half-siblings warned plaintiffs "that Lisa was up to something regarding Ron's song catalogue, which prompted [Plaintiffs] to investigate." In early 2019, plaintiffs discovered existence of allegedly invalid termination notices via Copyright Office's records." In March 2019, plaintiffs notified Sony that termination notices were invalid, unenforceable, and ineffective. Lisa eventually signed publishing deal with Sony and began releasing her own re-recordings of Ron's songs in April 2019. Plaintiffs sought declaration that 38 termination notices were invalid, ineffective, and unenforceable because Lisa did not have right to exercise them on behalf of Aurora and because notices failed to comply with statutory requirements under Copyright Act. Court noted that three-year statute of limitations found in § 507(b) apples to copyright ownership claims, which accrue "when plain and express repudiation" of ownership is communicated to claimant, and are barred three years from time of repudiation. Claims tied to termination-notice issues are treated as ownership claims, and are thus subject to that repudiation-based focus. Complaint itself revealed that, before September 7, 2020 (i.e., three years before plaintiffs filed complaint), plaintiffs had: (1) been warned by Lisa's half-siblings that Lisa was "up to something," which caused plaintiffs to investigate; (2) discovered existence of notices via Copyright Office's records; (3) notified Sony that termination notices were invalid, unenforceable, and ineffective; and (4) after months of attempting to reach resolution with Lisa, been met with behavior from Lisa where she "became obstinate, refusing to answer basic questions or provide documents about the Invalid Termination Notices, including the alleged basis for Lisa's authority to send the Invalid Termination Notices on behalf of Aurora." Plaintiffs argued that law required any repudiation to have been communicated to them *by* Lisa, not simply that plaintiffs acquired information that led to potential ownership dispute. Court disagreed; under Ninth Circuit law "claims of co-ownership … accrue when plain and express repudiation of co-ownership is communicated to the claimant, and are barred three years from the time of repudiation." Plaintiffs could have taken action, but did not do so—possibly, court noted, because plaintiffs may have hoped out-of-court resolution could have been obtained. But "possession of a hope does not excuse inaction." Court accordingly dismissed plaintiffs' declaratory relief claim with prejudice.

Crabtree v. Kirkman, No. 22-180, 2023 U.S. Dist. LEXIS 209380 (C.D. Cal. Nov. 22, 2023)

Court granted defendants' motion to dismiss plaintiff's copyright claims as barred by statute of limitations. Plaintiff worked as colorist for comic book series *Invincible*. Defendant was writer and co-creator of *Invincible*. In 2005, defendant had plaintiff sign Certificate of Authorship stating *Invincible* was work for hire owned by defendant. In 2012, plaintiff became aware that digital versions of single issue of *Invincible* were being sold online (not contemplated when initial agreement signed). Plaintiff believed he should be entitled to payment and emailed defendant. Defendant told plaintiff that plaintiff had signed work for hire agreement and was not owed royalties. He also explained digital issue sales were not single-issue sales that would entitle plaintiff to royalties. In 2020, plaintiff learned of Amazon TV series based on *Invincible* and asked for royalties. After defendant declined, plaintiff filed suit. Court found three-year statute of limitations barred plaintiff's claim seeking declaratory relief that he was co-author and accounting. Claims of co-authorship accrue when plain and express repudiation of co-ownership is communicated to claimant. Court found conversations in 2012 were clear repudiation of plaintiff's ownership interest sufficient for statute of limitations to accrue. In emails and phone calls in 2012, defendant made clear his view that digital editions should not be treated as single issue sales to receive royalties. Defendant also made repeated references to "work for hire" contract plaintiff signed, indicating plaintiff did not own copyright and that defendant (who commissioned work) was sole author and owner of copyright. Equitable estoppel did not apply because plaintiff failed to point to anything that occurred after 2012 conversations that "lulled him into inaction."

Dermansky v. Young Turks, Inc., No. 23-5868, 2023 U.S. Dist. LEXIS 199258 (C.D. Cal. Nov. 3, 2023)

District court granted in part defendant's motion to dismiss. Plaintiff professional commercial photographer provided photography services to clients and licensed photos for use. Five photographs at issue were allegedly taken by plaintiff between 2018 and 2020 and used by defendant The Young Turks in online news videos. Each photograph was licensed to and published on DesmogBlog.com with plaintiff's watermark containing CMI. Plaintiff alleged four claims: (1) direct copyright infringement; (2) contributory infringement of EPA photograph; (3) removal and/or alteration of plaintiff's CMI from photographs; and (4) falsely displaying defendant's own CMI on photographs. Defendant moved to dismiss portions of first and third claims and second and fourth claims in their entirety. Court denied motion to dismiss first and third claims, stating motion to dismiss must be directed to entire claim. Regarding second claim, court noted copyright infringement claim accrues—and statute of limitations begins to run—when party discovers, or reasonably should have discovered, alleged infringement. Here, initial infringing act occurred when defendant posted EPA video, with plaintiff's EPA photograph, in May 2017. Plaintiff's exhibit and screenshot showed EPA video was viewed in January 2018, more than three years before filing of complaint. Question raised by motion was whether defendant committed successive violation within three-year statute of limitations period. Court rejected plaintiff's argument that defendant's failure to remove EPA video and its continued receipt of advertising revenue from its posting constituted separately accruing harm. Sole infringing act was defendant's posting video on its YouTube channel. While failure to remove video may have caused continuing harm, inaction does not constitute discrete infringing act that caused injury beyond initial posting. Because plaintiff knew of infringing act more than three years before filing, and because plaintiff failed to allege discrete act that would create separately accruing harm, court dismissed second claim as untimely. Fourth claim dismissed because abandoned by plaintiff.

Williams v. Bobo, No. 22-3561, 2023 U.S. Dist. LEXIS 128798 (S.D. Ohio July 25, 2023)

District court denied defendants' motion to dismiss plaintiff's infringement claims, finding that licensing agreement between plaintiff and defendant did not constitute "direct repudiation" of plaintiff's ownership and authorship claims for purposes of claim accrual, so statute of limitations had not expired. Plaintiff collaborated with defendant Bobo to produce popular card game "Black Card Revoked" ("Work"), which became "leading American black culture trivia game in the United States," and inspired television show and spin-off games. Bobo formed defendant Zahara Ariel LLC to monetize Work, and plaintiff and Bobo formed defendant MTF Partners LLC to commercialize Work for television. To effectuate this arrangement, Zahara and MTF entered into agreement, which stated that Zahara was "sole and exclusive owner of a copyright and trademark portfolio" of Work, but included no assignment of ownership or authorship rights to Zahara. Plaintiff sought "declaratory judgment of copyright authorship"; defendants moved to dismiss. Court noted that it was not clear that plaintiff was asserting copyright *ownership* claim. However, whether and how much plaintiff could recover on some remedies she sought depended on whether she had ownership rights. "Therefore, the Court will consider whether Plaintiff's ownership claim—if she asserts such a claim—is barred by the statute of limitations." Defendants argued that plaintiff's claims accrued when plaintiff's claims of ownership and authorship of Work were directly repudiated by language in agreement describing Zahara as owner of Work. Court disagreed with defendants, finding that Zahara had no "competing claim of ownership," as there had been no assignment from plaintiff and/or Bobo to Zahara, so only Bobo, and not Zahara, could have directly repudiated plaintiff's claim. Although Bobo signed Agreement, it was in capacity as representative of Zahara, so statements in Agreement could not be repudiation by Bobo. Motion to dismiss denied on basis that Agreement did not constitute direct repudiation of plaintiff's authorship and ownership claims.

Stokes v. Brinor, Inc., No. 22-973, 2023 U.S. Dist. LEXIS 123840 (N.D. Oh. July 18, 2023)

District court denied summary judgment motion, seeking to limit statutory damages to three years. Plaintiff accused defendant saloon of displaying flyer on its Facebook page containing altered version of plaintiff's photograph. Plaintiff sued for infringement, seeking statutory damages. Defendant sought summary judgment on statute of limitations. Though Facebook post was from 2016—more than three years before suit was filed in 2022—court applied discovery rule and found no evidence that plaintiff should have been aware of post any sooner than its discovery in 2022. Defendant then argued that statutory damages should be limited to three years preceding complaint, but court found that case law putting three year bar on actual damages did not affect statutory damages. Court also denied summary judgment for both parties on amount of statutory damages, finding that genuine dispute of fact remained as to whether defendant acted willfully.

LeSEA, Inc. v. LeSEA Broad. Corp., No. 18-914, 2023 U.S. Dist. LEXIS 148026 (N.D. Ind. Aug. 22, 2023)

District court held that plaintiff's infringement claim was one of ownership and therefore was time-barred. Prior to his 1996 death, Christian missionary, Dr. Sumrall, produced numerous publications and broadcasts, many of which were registered in his name or by his nonprofit entities. Dr. Sumrall's will, which was never probated, left his personal property to his three sons but did not address intellectual property. In 2005, all copyrights in Dr. Sumrall's written works were assigned to defendant, ministry-controlled broadcasting company. Also in 2005, one of Dr. Sumrall's sons, Frank, empowered his own son, Lester, to receive one-third interest in personal property bequeathed by Dr. Sumrall. In 2017, Lester, acting on Frank's behalf pursuant to 2005 power of attorney, petitioned to probate Dr. Sumrall's will, arguing that Dr. Sumrall was owner of intellectual property from which defendants were profiting. District court held that central dispute in this case was one of copyright ownership, rather than infringement, meaning that claim accrued either shortly after Dr. Sumrall's death in 1996 (when Frank was advised that Dr. Sumrall had left everything to ministry) or at least in 2005 (when Frank authorized Lester to recover previously-denied one-third share of Dr. Sumrall's estate), and therefore copyright claim, filed in 2018, was time-barred.

C. Res Judicata/Collateral Estoppel

Crabtree v. Kirkman, No. 22-180, 2023 U.S. Dist. LEXIS 209380 (C.D. Cal. Nov. 22, 2023)

Court granted defendants' motion to dismiss plaintiff's copyright claims as barred by statute of limitations. Plaintiff worked as colorist for comic book series *Invincible*. Defendant was writer and co-creator of *Invincible*. In 2005, defendant had plaintiff sign Certificate of Authorship stating *Invincible* was work for hire owned by defendant. In 2012, plaintiff became aware that digital versions of single issue of *Invincible* were being sold online (not contemplated when initial agreement signed). Plaintiff believed he should be entitled to payment and emailed defendant. Defendant told plaintiff that plaintiff had signed work for hire agreement and was not owed royalties. He also explained digital issue sales were not single-issue sales that would entitle plaintiff to royalties. In 2020, plaintiff learned of Amazon TV series based on *Invincible* and asked for royalties. After defendant declined, plaintiff filed suit. Court found three-year statute of limitations barred plaintiff's claim seeking declaratory relief that he was co-author and accounting. Claims of co-authorship accrue when plain and express repudiation of co-ownership is communicated to claimant. Court found conversations in 2012 were clear repudiation of plaintiff's ownership interest sufficient for statute of limitations to accrue. In emails and phone calls in 2012, defendant made clear his view that digital editions should not be treated as single issue sales to receive royalties. Defendant also made repeated references to "work for hire" contract plaintiff signed, indicating plaintiff did not own copyright and that defendant (who commissioned work) was sole author and owner of copyright. Equitable estoppel did not apply because plaintiff failed to point to anything that occurred after 2012 conversations that "lulled him into inaction."

D. Miscellaneous

Trent P. Fisher Enters., LLC v. SAS Automation, LLC, No. 20-216, 2023 U.S. Dist. LEXIS 135933 (S.D. Ohio Aug. 3, 2023)

District court denied plaintiffs' motion for summary judgment on defendants' affirmative open-source defense. Plaintiffs sold defendant SAS to defendants Piab USA, Inc. and Piab AB. As part of transaction, plaintiffs transferred equity in SAS to Piab, but Piab assigned IP rights in SAS's proprietary e-commerce software ("Works") to plaintiffs to be licensed back to Piab. Works were developed in significant part with code from open-source e-commerce software OpenCart pursuant to GNU General Public License ("GPL"), obliging developers to publicly disclose source code and make work available for free use if software developed via GPL is "covered work" and "conveyed" to third party. When Piab developed in-house e-commerce software largely based on source code from

Works, plaintiff sued alleged infringement. Plaintiffs moved for summary judgment, requesting that court reject defendants' affirmative defense that Works are open-source and covered by GPL. Works which are "combined" with GPL source code are covered by GPL. In rejecting plaintiffs' motion, court found that reasonable factfinder could conclude Works were "combined" with GPL source code, since Works substantially relied on integration with OpenCart, and that license from Fisher to Piab constituted "conveyance" of Works. As such, genuine issues of material fact remained on question whether Works were covered by GPL.

Cooley v. Marcus, No. 23-86, 2023 U.S. Dist. LEXIS 127119 (W.D. Mich. July 24, 2023)

District court granted in part and denied in part defendant's motion to dismiss complaint. According to complaint, defendant posted video to GoFundMe fundraising page that featured photos and video recordings of Elle Roskamp, defendant's sister, who was missing person. Approximately 17 months later, plaintiff registered copyright in several photos and videos appearing in plaintiff's GoFundMe video. Defendant asserted defense of *de minimis* use. Regarding *de minimis* use, district court concluded that plaintiffs appeared to be claiming defendant copied plaintiffs' entire works, and that plaintiffs' works appeared prominently and clearly in defendant's video, filling most of screen and without blurring. District court rejected defendant's argument that subject works were only displayed for few seconds in defendant's video, because works at issue were displayed with sufficient detail for viewers to readily identify details of plaintiffs' works. District court therefore denied defendant's attempt to dismiss complaint based on alleged *de minimis* use.

VII. REMEDIES

A. Damages and Profits

Warner Chappell Music, Inc. v. Nealy, No. 22-1078, 601 U.S. ___ (2024)

Supreme Court resolved question of lookback period for computing damages, rejecting Second Circuit's decision in *Sohm v. Scholastic, Inc.*, 959 F.3d 39 (2d Cir. 2020), limiting recovery to three years immediately preceding filing of suit, and holding that Copyright Act contains no separate time-based limit on monetary recovery. Plaintiff Sherman Nealy and Tony Butler formed music company, Music Specialist, Inc., in 1983. Company had little success and dissolved after few years. Nealy then served prison terms in 1989-2008 and 2012-2015 for drug-related offenses. During this period, Butler entered into licenses of company's works to Warner Chappell, several of which were incorporated into hit recordings as well as TV series. Nealy claimed to be copyright owner of works at issue, and that he was unaware of these uses until 2016, shortly after end of his second prison term. In 2018, he commenced infringement action and sought damages going back to 2008. In district court, Warner Chappell accepted that Nealy's claims were timely under discovery rule, but urged court to limit lookback period for damages to three years prior to suit. Court agreed, citing *Sohm*. On interlocutory appeal, Eleventh Circuit reversed, following Ninth Circuit's contrary ruling in *Starz Entertainment v. MGM*, 39 F.3d 1236 (9th Cir. 2022). Certified question for interlocutory appeal did not challenge discovery rule itself, but only application of lookback for purposes of determining damages; it "assumed for purposes of answering" this question that all of Nealy's claims were timely under discovery rule. Supreme Court granted *certiorari* on question "whether, under the discovery accrual rule applied by the circuit courts, a copyright plaintiff can recover damages for acts that allegedly occurred more than three years before the filing of a lawsuit." Supreme Court acknowledged that it was assuming, but not deciding, that discovery rule was valid interpretation of three-year accrual language in § 507(b). Majority, in opinion by Justice Kagan (joined by Chief Justice Roberts and Justices Sotomayor, Kavanaugh, Barrett and Jackson) noted that *Petrella v. MGM, Inc.*, 572 U.S. 663 (2014), did not in fact decide either discovery rule or lookback rule, because plaintiff in *Petrella* had known of alleged infringements for many years. Therefore, plaintiff in *Petrella* "could not avail herself of discovery rule" and "sued only for infringements that occurred in the three years before her suit." *Petrella* did not "go beyond case's facts" to resolve question presented in *Nealy*, or broader issue of whether discovery rule is valid interpretation of § 507(b). Majority noted that Warner Chappell had not challenged discovery rule itself in district court or Eleventh Circuit; thus issue was not properly before Court. Having thus confined its opinion to lookback question, majority found Act fails to impose time limit on lookback even as it specifies three-year "time-to-sue prescription" in § 507(b). Therefore, "if any time limit on damages exists, it must come from the Act's remedial sections," § 504(a)-(c), and those provisions include no such time limit on recoverable damages for timely claims. Lack of textual support for limiting lookback period led majority to reject Second Circuit's conclusion in *Sohm*, as did fact that *Sohm* view was "essentially self-defeating." Majority thus affirmed Eleventh Circuit. Dissent by Justice Gorsuch (joined by Justices Thomas and Alito) took exception to majority's willingness to assume, without deciding, that discovery rule is permissible reading of three-year accrual language in § 507(b). Dissent argued that Act "almost certainly does not tolerate a discovery rule" because, as *Petrella* notes, claim ordinarily accrues when plaintiff has "complete and present cause of action … In other words, … when plaintiff can file suit and obtain relief." Dissent described this as traditional "incident of injury rule," and stated that unless statute directs otherwise, "we proceed consistent with traditional equitable practice and ordinarily apply the discovery rule 'only in cases of fraud or concealment.'" Under "standard rule," dissent continued, "discovery rule has no role to play here—or, indeed, in the mine run of copyright cases," where there is no allegation of fraud or concealment that would entitle plaintiff to equitable tolling. Dissent concluded that Court may, as it does, resolve parties' dispute while leaving for another day antecedent question whether discovery rule exists under Act. "But if that is a permissible course, it does not strike me as the most sensible one. … Respectfully, rather than devote our time to this case, I would have dismissed it as improvidently granted and awaited another squarely presenting the question whether the Copyright Act authorizes the discovery rule. Better, in my view, to answer a question that does matter than one that almost certainly does not."

Reiffer v. NYC Luxury Limousine Ltd., No. 22-2374, 2023 U.S. Dist. LEXIS 104552 (S.D.N.Y. June 15, 2023)

District court awarded statutory damages to prevailing plaintiff after summary judgment. Defendant, limousine business, displayed and removed copyright management information from photograph of New York skyline taken by plaintiff, photographer. Defendant admitted some (but not all) elements of plaintiff's claim in its answer. Defendant did not participate in court-ordered mediation nor respond to document requests or interrogatories until ordered to do so by court. By never responding to plaintiff's requests to admit, defendant also admitted all factual assertions therein. Defendant expressly admitted facts in plaintiff's summary judgment statement of facts, and offered one "fact" in its response, namely, that defendant had promptly removed infringing image from its website, but cited only to defendant's unverified answer. In its summary judgment opposition, defendant conceded liability with respect to plaintiff's claims and argued only concerning measure of damages, speculating that plaintiff would have accepted minimal amount, "say $500 or $1000," rather than $8,500 established as licensing fee by undisputed evidence. In holding that plaintiff entitled to statutory damages, court found that defendant's infringement was willful because defendant had conceded that it had intentionally deleted plaintiff's name from photograph before posting it to defendant's website. Defendant's uncooperativeness in discovery and dismissive litigation conduct, as well as need for deterrence, weighed in favor of $30,500 statutory damages award.

Trent P. Fisher Enters., LLC v. SAS Automation, LLC, No. 20-216, 2023 U.S. Dist. LEXIS 135933 (S.D. Ohio Aug. 3, 2023)

District court denied defendants' request for limitation of damages on plaintiffs' infringement claim. Plaintiffs sold defendant SAS to defendants Piab USA, Inc. and Piab AB. As part of transaction, plaintiffs transferred equity in SAS to Piab, but Piab assigned IP rights in SAS's proprietary e-commerce software ("Works") to plaintiffs to be licensed back to Piab. Works were developed in significant part with code from open-source e-commerce software OpenCart pursuant to GNU General Public License ("GPL"), obliging developers to publicly disclose source code and make work available for free use if software developed via GPL is "covered work" and "conveyed" to third party. When Piab developed in-house e-commerce software largely based on source code from Works, plaintiff sued alleging copyright infringement. Defendants requested limitation of damages on basis that plaintiffs had not shown that requested damages were "reasonably related" to Works, as online sales made via Works were tracked by OpenCart, and such sales were well below plaintiffs' requested damages. In denying defendants' motion, court found that, while requested damages were greater than online sales revenue connected to Works, genuine issues of material fact remained as to extent to which Works contributed to defendants' offline revenue.

> *Nat'l Presto Indus. v. United States Merchs. Fin. Grp., Inc.*, No. 18-3321, 2023 U.S. Dist. LEXIS 206092 (D. Minn. Nov. 17, 2023)

Court denied defendant's motion for judgment as matter of law or for new trial on plaintiff's infringement claim regarding user manual. Plaintiff Presto manufactured electric heater called HeatDish and sold it exclusively to Costco. In 2017, Costco sought new heater supplier. Defendant U.S. Merchants contacted suppliers and obtained samples of plaintiff's HeatDish and by late 2017, developed its own heater, The Heat Machine, and sold to Costco. Original manual for The Heat Machine had similar language to plaintiff's 1995 HeatDish manual. After plaintiff sued for copyright infringement in December 2018, defendant continued selling heaters with original manual for several more weeks before revising it. Following jury trial, plaintiff awarded $150,000 in statutory damages for defendant's copyright infringement. Defendant filed instant motion for judgment as matter of law, new trial, or remittitur. Court analyzed whether jury could reasonably infer that defendant copied 1995 HeatDish manual and whether infringement was willful, and answered both affirmatively. Parties did not dispute copying, but whether defendant, versus its overseas manufacturer, was legally responsible for copying that occurred. Reasonable jury could find defendants engaged in volitional conduct when it edited substantively first draft of Heat Machine manual for style and formatting. Court refused to overturn jury's finding of willfulness where it found large portions of Heat Machine text manual identical to 1995 HeatDish manual, defendant changed language of draft manual to change how closely it mirrored 1995 manual, and included language in manual that did not match product specifications (suggesting it came from another source). Together, facts showed willfulness. Court denied defendant's motion for JMOL or new trial.

B. Attorneys' Fees

> *Poppington, LLC v. Brooks*, No. 23-660, 2024 U.S. App. LEXIS 7112 (2d Cir. Mar. 26, 2024)

Second circuit affirmed award of $44,496.05 in attorneys' fees to defendant following dismissal of infringement complaint on summary judgment. Defendant author hired plaintiffs to create short film relating to her *Mafietta* series of novellas, and during filming plaintiffs also took photographs on set during filming. After defendant later published book including photographs taken by plaintiffs, plaintiffs sued for infringement. Following discovery, district court granted summary judgment to defendant "on the ground that the photograph was a derivative work of the *Mafietta* film," and defendant moved for attorneys' fees and costs. Second Circuit noted that district court conducted "particularized, case-by-case assessment" of fee request, and found that plaintiff's suit was "meritless and the reasons for bringing it were retaliatory," thus favoring fee award. Finding that district court did not abuse discretion in considering *Fogerty* and *Kirtsaeng* factors in determining fee award, district court judgment affirmed.

Gaede v. Delay, Nos. 23-35217, 23-35531, 2024 U.S. App. LEXIS 5389 (9th Cir. Mar. 6, 2024)

Ninth Circuit affirmed with-prejudice dismissal of complaint and award of attorneys' fees, but reversed as to amount of fees. District court had properly dismissed plaintiffs' complaint because their copyright infringement claims, as they conceded, were predicated upon ideas rather than expressions thereof. Plaintiffs' repeated efforts to assert their claims could therefore reasonably be characterized as "unreasonable, if not frivolous." As such, award of attorneys' fees was appropriate and, further, billed hourly rates were reasonable. However, Ninth Circuit held that district court had abused its discretion in awarding fees that may have been attributable to legal advice provided to defendant's principals individually, rather than to defendant itself.

Lowery v. Rhapsody Int'l, Inc., 75 F.4th 985 (9th Cir. 2023)

Ninth Circuit found district court's attorneys' fees award of $1.7 million in class action infringement suit unreasonable in case which led to only $53,000 in class recovery, and reversed and remanded for consideration of fee award. Plaintiff musical composition copyright owners sued Rhapsody (subsequently rebranded to Napster) in 2016 on behalf of purported class alleging infringement by reproducing and distributing musical compositions without obtaining voluntary or compulsory license. During pendency of litigation, Rhapsody negotiated separate settlement with National Music Publishers Association (NMPA) concerning similar licensing claims, and to receive payment as part of that settlement, copyright owners had to waive right to make claims in this lawsuit. Also during pendency of litigation, Congress passed Music Modernization Act, which updated procedure for obtaining music licenses at issue in case. Parties ultimately reached settlement agreement under which Rhapsody would pay maximum of $20 million on class members' claims, but because NMPA settlement "gutted the potential class," very few claims were submitted and Rhapsody only paid about $53,000 to satisfy class members' claims. Applying "lodestar method" to determine fees award, district court awarded $1.7 million to "adequately reimburse[]" plaintiffs' counsel for their work, and in so doing "declined to place a value on the benefit to the class." On appeal Ninth Circuit found fee award not reasonable, reversed and remanded with instructions for district court to "justify any fee award it makes by comparing it to the benefit provided to the class." Ninth Circuit rejected reliance on hypothetical $20 million settlement cap in calculating fee, noting that parties should have been aware in view of NMPA settlement that "there was no realistic possibility that the actual payout to class members would approach anywhere near $20 million." Ninth Circuit further directed district court to conduct "cross check" of its lodestar calculation against percentage of recovery calculation method, noting that amounts exceeding 25% of settlement value are "major red flag that signifies that lawyers are being overcompensated." Ninth Circuit distinguished civil rights cases, where monetary damage awards tend to be low but "benefit to society through nonmonetary relief" can be high and thus justify disproportionate attorneys' fees awards, from copyright cases, which tend to lack substantial nonmonetary relief or meaningful benefit to society. Reversed and remanded with instructions to "determine the class action settlement's actual value to the class members."

> *UIRC-GSA Holdings, LLC v. William Blair & Co., LLC*, Nos. 23-1527, 23-2566, 2024 U.S. App. LEXIS 6500 (7th Cir. Mar. 19, 2024)

Seventh Circuit granted defendants' motion for attorneys' fees incurred on appeal. Plaintiff real estate company, which raised money by issuing bonds, prepared bond offering documents ("Works") largely copied from third party source and registered Works with Copyright Office. Plaintiff later hired defendant to bring bond offerings to market. Defendant was hired by another party to draft bond documents and defendant copied portions of Works to prepare such documents, prompting plaintiff to sue for copyright infringement. District court granted defendant's motion for summary judgment and motion for attorneys' fees. Plaintiff appealed, and Seventh Circuit affirmed, holding that copyrights in Works were invalid, and that district court did not abuse its discretion by granting defendant's motion for fees associated with district court phase of litigation. Appeals court weighed factors in making attorneys' fees determination: "(1) the frivolousness of the suit; (2) the losing party's motivation for bringing or defendant against a suit; (3) the objective unreasonableness of the claims advanced by the losing party; and (4) the need to advance considerations of compensation and deterrence." As to frivolousness factor, defendant argued plaintiff "litigate[d] a copyright case (for years) based on material that it knew it did not draft," but appeals court noted plaintiff did in fact draft some of Works and suit was not frivolous. Court also found motivation and objective unreasonableness factors favored neither party, but "compensation and deterrence" factor favored defendant because "not awarding fees might deter defendants like [defendant] from defending cases." Court also approved full amount requested by defendant, which was calculated using lodestar rate and based on defendant's attorneys' actual billing records.

Live Face on Web, LLC v. Cremation Soc'y of Ill., Inc., 77 F.4th 630 (7th Cir. 2023)

Seventh Circuit reversed denial of attorneys' fees to prevailing copyright infringement defendants. District court declined to award attorneys' fees to prevailing, noting that defendants prevailed only due to intervening Supreme Court decision in *Google LLC v. Oracle America, Inc.*, 141 S. Ct. 1183 (2021), which came down after plaintiff filed complaint, causing plaintiff to withdraw its own complaint. District court found that awarding fees would not advance purposes of Copyright Act's fee-shifting provision, such as deterrence and punishing frivolous and unreasonable claims. Seventh Circuit disagreed, finding that those factors were outweighed by very strong presumption in favor of awarding fees to victorious copyright defendants, because asymmetric recoveries allow victorious plaintiff to recover damages even if no fees are awarded, but victorious defendant will not obtain damages and thus must obtain fees in order to break even. Seventh Circuit also noted defendants prevailed not just because of Supreme Court decision, but because of their defenses, which might have prevailed even if this case were decided before Supreme Court *Google* decision. Seventh Circuit was also unconvinced that Google case was dispositive on this case, as plaintiff withdrew without testing its theory. Seventh Circuit further found plaintiff, who filed hundreds of similar suits, to be copyright troll, disagreeing with district court's opinion to contrary.

Markham Concepts v. Hasbro, Inc., 71 F.4th 80 (1st Cir. 2023)

First Circuit affirmed district court's denial of attorneys' fees to prevailing defendants. Case arose from dispute between toy developer who came up with initial concept for "The Game of Life" before it was introduced in 1960 by Milton Bradley Company and game designer who developer recruited to design and create actual game prototype. After game's success, designer felt he was not given proper recognition and that royalties were too low. Game designer's successors-in-interest sued defendant toy developer and others seeking to renegotiate original assignment of rights in game. District court analyzed whether game designer created prototype such (and could be considered its author) and whether it was work made for hire. District court concluded prototype was work for hire created for defendant and designer was not author for copyright purposes, thereby foreclosing successors-in-interest from terminating assignment agreement. District court relied on "instance and expense" test to determine whether game was work for hire. District court considered non-exhaustive *Fogerty* factors in denying defendants' request for attorneys' fees. First Circuit held that district court did not abuse its discretion by denying defendants attorneys' fees from unsuccessful plaintiffs where both sides raised plausible arguments and plaintiffs' claim was not so weak as to be objectively unreasonable.

Applicable law as to plaintiffs' copyright claim was not so black and white that district court acted unjustifiably when it deemed their argument against "instance and expense" test to be "within the realm of reasonableness." In addition, there was enough ambiguity in evidence on how board game prototype was created, as well as on understanding about who should be designated as prototype's author, that First Circuit could not reject district court's view that plaintiffs' factual position was not wholly unreasonable. Court declined to override district court's assessment of plaintiffs' factual case, particularly in absence of findings and ruling on defendants' alternative theory for classifying prototype as work for hire. Court found no flaw in district court's brief treatment of motivation and deterrence *Fogerty* factors despite defendants' argument that district court erred in "summarily discounting" them. It was reasonable district court would find no need for additional deterrence because result of its ruling meant plaintiffs had no choice but to live with assignment agreement designer reached in 1959. First Circuit also declined to award fees for appeal, citing similar support as district court. Most factors played out similarly, in particular reasonableness of plaintiffs' argument that case law discredited "instance and expense" test for identifying work for hire under 1909 Act. Plaintiffs' argument was not objectively unreasonable. Court thought defendants faced "higher hurdle" with respect to factual reasonableness of their appeal challenging district court's finding that "The Game of Life" prototype was work for hire for game designer. Court concluded that *Fogerty* unreasonableness factor, due "substantial weight," did not favor imposing responsibility for defendants' attorneys' fees on plaintiffs. Court rejected defendants' argument that plaintiffs' motivation was "driven solely by greed or animosity towards" toy developer. Court highlighted statutory termination right as one established to allow authorities to renegotiate terms, financial and otherwise, of early assignment of rights—plausibly what plaintiffs attempted to do here. Court again stated it did not believe fee award for appellate-level proceedings would serve deterrence objective (for these plaintiffs or others).

Atticus Ltd. Liab. Co. v. Dramatic Publ'g Co., No. 22-10147, 2023 U.S. Dist. LEXIS 195527 (S.D.N.Y. Oct. 31, 2023)

District court granted in part plaintiff's motion for attorneys' fees. Court found as matter of law that defendant did not have exclusive rights to amateur productions of play derived from Harper Lee's novel *To Kill a Mockingbird.* Declaratory plaintiff moved for attorneys' fees. Court noted it may consider several nonexclusive factors in making fees determination, namely, "frivolousness, motivation, objective unreasonableness, and the need in particular circumstances to advance considerations of compensation and deterrence." Plaintiff argued defendant's litigation positions were objectively unreasonable, as defendant's argument that exclusive licenses are interminable was "nonsensical" and contrary to unambiguous provision in Copyright Act; defendant pressed for needless discovery in pursuit of its unfounded speculation that plaintiff controlled Lee's estate in estate's arbitration with defendant; and defendant's resort to statute of limitations bar was unfounded. Relatedly, plaintiff alleged aforementioned conduct unnecessarily prolonged litigation. Court found that, while defendant's argument that exclusive licenses are interminable under § 304(c) was legally untenable, it was not unreasonable for defendant to argue such because defendant already prevailed in arbitration on basis of same argument and arbitration award was being appealed, so it was reasonable for defendant to rely on argument. Accordingly, court declined to award fees in connection with argument that exclusive licenses are not subject to termination. However, court agreed defendant needlessly and unreasonably prolonged litigation, and that defendant's arguments regarding statute of limitations and plaintiff's control of estate were "unintelligible" and "far-fetched, untethered to any reliable evidence," respectively. Court also found fee award would advance public interest because it would allow public access to multiple stage plays based on novel. Accordingly, court awarded partial attorneys' fees to plaintiff.

Paulo v. Agence France Presse, No. 21-11209, 2023 U.S. Dist. LEXIS 207171 (S.D.N.Y. Oct. 17, 2023)

Magistrate judge recommended denial of defendants' motion for attorneys' fees and costs. Portuguese photojournalist Leong Francisco Paulo sued Agence France Presse (AFP) and two Getty Images corporate entities for infringement and violations of CMI. Related litigation also commenced in Portuguese court. District court conditionally dismissed claims filed in Southern District of New York based on *forum non conveniens* and lack of personal jurisdiction, on condition that defendants agree to submit to jurisdiction of Portuguese court. On motion for fees and costs, magistrate concluded that dismissal for *forum non conveniens* did not establish defendants as prevailing parties, necessary condition to obtain attorneys' fees and costs. Dismissal for lack of personal jurisdiction also did not transform defendants into prevailing parties, because decision did not insulate defendants from risk of future litigation; indeed, condition of dismissal was that plaintiff remained free to bring claims against AFP in Portugal. Defendants therefore failed to establish necessary condition of prevailing party. Defendants also sought costs under 28 U.S.C. § 1919, which allows for award of costs when dismissal is for lack of jurisdiction. However, district court noted that dismissal on *forum non conveniens* grounds does not constitute lack of jurisdiction. Though dismissal for lack of personal jurisdiction could allow for costs under § 1919, district court concluded that discretionary factors weighed against awarding costs. Finally, though Rule 41(d)(1) allows for fees incurred when plaintiff dismisses action and then refiles against same defendant, district court held that Rule 41(d)(1) applies to litigation within United States that was previously dismissed by plaintiff, not extraterritorial litigation.

Id Tech. LLC v. Toggle Web Media LLC, No. 20-5949, 2023 U.S. Dist. LEXIS 182266 (E.D.N.Y. Oct. 10, 2023)

Magistrate judge recommended district court grant defendants' motion for attorneys' fees. Plaintiff and defendants sold custom jewelry on Internet. Plaintiff alleged defendants infringed copyright by creating website substantially similar and virtually indistinguishable from plaintiff's. Court granted defendants' motion to dismiss. Defendants requested attorneys' fees. Judge found plaintiff's infringement claim objectively unreasonable because plaintiff did not have copyright registration and failed to point to specific infringing elements of defendants' website that may have been protected by copyrights. Judge found award of reasonable attorneys' fees for defendants appropriate. Considering defendants' counsel's past experience and substantive nature of work on case, judge found requested hourly rate reasonable. Magistrate judge found time spent reasonable, but records included vague and unnecessary entries, so recommended reducing requested hours by five percent. Magistrate judge recommended awarding defendants court's filing fee because fee appeared on docket.

Reiffer v. NYC Luxury Limousine Ltd., No. 22-2374, 2023 U.S. Dist. LEXIS 104552 (S.D.N.Y. June 15, 2023)

District court found prevailing plaintiff entitled to attorneys' fees after grant of summary judgment. Defendant, limousine business, displayed and removed copyright management information from photograph of New York skyline taken by plaintiff, photographer. Defendant admitted some (but not all) elements of plaintiff's claim in its answer. Defendant did not participate in court-ordered mediation nor respond to document requests or interrogatories until ordered to do so by court. By never responding to plaintiff's requests to admit, defendant also admitted all factual assertions therein. Defendant expressly admitted facts in plaintiff's summary judgment statement of facts, and offered one "fact" in its response, namely, that defendant had promptly removed infringing image from its website, but cited only to defendant's unverified answer. In its summary judgment opposition, defendant conceded liability with respect to plaintiff's claims and argued only concerning measure of damages, speculating that plaintiff would have accepted minimal amount, "say $500 or $1000," rather than $8,500 established as licensing fee by undisputed evidence. Plaintiff entitled to attorneys' fees because defendant's position in litigation was objectively unreasonable, including because defendant failed to fully concede liability in his answer, thereby necessitating discovery. Defendant also asserted affirmative defenses for which it had no factual basis. Defendant's cavalier attitude weighed in favor of attorneys' fees award. Court directed plaintiff to submit attorneys' fees motion.

Russell v. Walmart Inc., No. 19-5495, 2024 U.S. Dist. LEXIS 15631 (C.D. Cal. Jan. 2, 2024)

District court granted plaintiff's motion for attorneys' fees but for less than amount sought. Plaintiff filed copyright infringement action alleging that defendant infringed copyrighted photographs by storing photographs on servers and displaying copies on defendant's website, and that defendant infringed copyrighted sculptures by selling replicas. Jury found in favor of plaintiff and plaintiff filed motion for attorneys' fees. Court found plaintiff prevailed on copyright claims and claims were clearly neither frivolous nor unreasonable nor pursued in bad faith. Court determined plaintiff's case furthered purposes of Copyright Act, and defendant asserted mostly meritless defenses throughout litigation. Court determined fee award would compensate plaintiff for work done in pursuing meritorious claims, especially those brought by small, independent artists against multibillion dollar corporations. Court found plaintiff obtained high degree of success by prevailing on all five infringement claims. Court held, based on totality of factors, plaintiff entitled to attorneys' fees. Court determined hourly rates were reasonable, and hours billed were reasonable, but modified amount for block billing. Court determined plaintiff entitled to attorneys' fees on both prevailing and non-prevailing claims because claims shared common core facts. Court exercised discretion to apply cut in light of plaintiff's failure to prevail on certain claims at trial.

Polychron v. Bezos, No. 23-2831, 2023 U.S. Dist. LEXIS 226148 (C.D. Cal. Dec. 14, 2023)

District court partially granted defendants' motion for attorneys' fees. Plaintiff Demetrious Polychron filed infringement and unfair competition claims against two Amazon companies, as well as entities and individual related to J.R.R. Tolkien estate. Plaintiff alleged defendants infringed his copyright in unauthorized derivative work that was based on defendants' registered work. Amazon defendants and Tolkien defendants each filed motions to dismiss, which were granted. In awarding attorneys' fees, district court looked to five non-exclusive Seltzer factors. First, plaintiff's action was dismissed in its entirety, with prejudice. Second, plaintiff's claim was frivolous because he alleged defendants had infringed plaintiff's copyright in unauthorized derivative work based on defendants' protected work. Third, defendants had informed plaintiff several times of flawed basis of his legal position, which, among other facts, suggested he may have had improper motivation in bringing suit. Fourth, district court noted it was objectively unreasonable for plaintiff to bring copyright claim after admitting he took his characters directly from defendants' protected work. Fifth, award of attorneys' fees would advance goals of general and specific deterrence. District court held that some of defendants' counsel billed too many hours in responding to complaint and amended complaint, and reduced number of hours accordingly. In sum, district court awarded $66,610 to Amazon defendants and $68,027 to Tolkien defendants.

Infogroup Inc. v. Office Depot, Inc., No. 23-80358, 2024 U.S. Dist. LEXIS 50246 (S.D. Fla. Mar. 12, 2024)

Plaintiff sued for infringement and related breach of contract claim relating to breach of licensing agreement for database directed at "direct marketing and internal research and analytics." After district court granted defendant's motion to dismiss infringement claim as preempted under license agreement (and further declining to exercise supplemental jurisdiction over state law breach of contract claim), defendant moved for attorneys' fees and costs as prevailing party. Magistrate judge recommended defendant's motion for fees and costs be denied, and defendant objected to magistrate's report. In considering magistrate's application of *Fogerty* factors, District Judge Aileen Cannon first analyzed defendant's assertion that magistrate "erred in not applying a presumption in favor of attorney's [sic] fees to the prevailing party." Finding that Eleventh Circuit does not apply such presumption and that magistrate applied proper neutral analysis to *Fogerty* factors, district court next turned to magistrate's analysis of factors themselves. On first and third factors (frivolousness and unreasonableness), district court agreed with magistrate that even though claim was dismissed under terms of license agreement, nothing in court's dismissal order characterized suit as frivolous or unreasonable. On "compensation and deterrence" factors, district court likewise found that magistrate adequately examined factor and property exercised its "wide latitude" to use discretion in declining to award costs and fees under. Motion for Attorneys' fees and costs under Act denied.

Infogroup Inc. v. Office Depot, Inc., No. 23-80358, 2023 U.S. Dist. LEXIS 197980 (S.D. Fla. Nov. 3, 2023)

District court denied defendant's motion for attorneys' fees under Copyright Act, finding plaintiff's interpretation of licensing agreement erroneous but not objectively unreasonable, and granted defendant attorneys' fees under Florida law, which governed interpretation of licensing agreement. Plaintiff data and technology provider originally brought complaint against defendant Office Depot alleging copyright infringement, believing defendant incorporated plaintiff's business database into mapping software program developed by defendant. Plaintiff later amended complaint to add breach of contract claim, alleging defendant's actions went beyond scope of parties' licensing agreement, which allowed for "direct marketing and internal research analytics." Plaintiff alleged defendant infringed its copyrights by using licensed data to allow defendant's real estate department to conduct real estate research and analytics. Plaintiff's amended complaint was dismissed; court rejected plaintiff's attempts to restrict broad language of licensing agreement and agreed with defendant that plain language of agreement did not restrict defendant's use of licensed data as plaintiff suggested. Defendant moved for attorneys' fees under both Copyright Act and licensing agreement. Court denied fees under Copyright Act. Documents produced during discovery revealed basis for plaintiff's good faith belief that defendant engaged in unauthorized use of its data. Court rejected defendant's argument that plaintiff's failure to address existence of licensing agreement in initial complaint showed lack of knowledge of licensing agreement or attempt to deceive court. Defendant cherry-picked deposition testimony that when read, in context, did not show plaintiff "admitting" that licensing agreement gave defendant license to use licensed data for its own direct marketing and internal research and analytics (as opposed to such use for purposes of direct marketing only). Finally, plaintiff's interpretation of licensing agreement was erroneous, but plausible. Court granted fees under licensing agreement because it did not limit recovery of attorneys' fees to breach of contract claims but extended to any litigation between parties with respect to licensing agreement.

Seventh Chakra Films, LLC v. Alesse, No. 21-21286, 2023 U.S. Dist. LEXIS 185481 (S.D. Fla. Oct. 15, 2023)

District court granted in part plaintiff's motion for attorneys' fees. Plaintiff film production company sought and obtained declaratory judgment confirming plaintiff's sole ownership of copyright in documentary film *1986: The Act* after defendant, former employee of plaintiff, filed state court action claiming 50 percent ownership of film. Plaintiff moved for attorneys' fees. Court noted that, as prevailing party, plaintiff was eligible for attorneys' fees. As to whether plaintiff was entitled to attorneys' fees, court, noting its broad discretion in fees awards, considered factors of (1) degree of success obtained; (2) frivolousness; (3) motivation; (4) objective unreasonableness (both in factual and legal components of case); and (5) need in particular circumstances to advance considerations of compensation and deterrence. Court found that factors 1, 2, 3, and 5 weighed in favor of fee award, while factor 4 carried less weight compared to other factors. Focusing on questions of frivolousness and objective unreasonableness, court found defendant's claim to ownership of work was without basis in fact or law, as defendant was employee of plaintiff; work was work made for hire; no written agreement to contrary existed; and plaintiff admitted defendant's owner was sole author of work. Court determined that attorneys' fees award was proper.

Sadowski v. Site Spin Off LLC, No. 23-297, 2023 U.S. Dist. LEXIS 124329 (M.D. Fla. July 19, 2023)

Plaintiff photographer sued defendant website operator for direct infringement, alleging defendant's website displayed copy of photograph showing "collection of small-packet condiment servings" on website article concerning nationwide shortage of ketchup packets. Following filing of complaint, defendant immediately removed photograph from website. In settlement discussions, plaintiff initially demanded $17,000, but then accepted defendant's $1,100 counter-offer; following entry of judgment in plaintiff's favor, plaintiff moved for $6,000 in attorneys' fees. Defendant opposed award of fees, arguing that (1) plaintiff is serial copyright litigant; (2) pre-litigation demand from plaintiff was sent to inactive email addresses; (3) plaintiff's settlement demand was exorbitant; and (4) plaintiff quickly accepted much lower offer of judgment. After finding plaintiff prevailing party, magistrate considered Fogerty factors in examining potential fee award. On frivolity/objective reasonableness factor, magistrate found plaintiff's claim neither frivolous nor objectively unreasonable, principally because parties agreed that plaintiff owned valid copyright in photograph and defendant posted photograph to its website without plaintiff's permission. On motivation factor, defendant emphasized that plaintiff was "serial copyright litigator," having filed over 167 cases nationwide, including 34 cases in past year. Defendant also argued that he never received plaintiff's purported pre-litigation notices, which were sent to inactive email addresses. Magistrate declined to infer bad faith on these facts, finding that plaintiff filing "numerous low value infringement cases is not necessarily evidence of bad faith," but rather may point to widespread infringement of plaintiff's works. On compensation and deterrence factor, magistrate likewise found plaintiff's claims reasonable and meritorious, and thus serve to further interests of Act. Magistrate thus found plaintiff entitled to claim post-judgment attorneys' fees under Local Rule and ordered supplemental briefs on calculation of award.

> *Affordable Aerial Photography, Inc. v. Prop. Matters United States, LLC*, No. 22-14296, 2023 U.S. Dist. LEXIS 115171 (S.D. Fla. July 5, 2023)

District court adopted magistrate judge's report and recommendations, denying defendant's motion for attorneys' fees and costs. When plaintiff voluntarily dismissed its infringement claims against defendant, without prejudice, defendant moved for attorneys' fees, arguing that it was "prevailing party" and "entitled to attorneys' fees in connection with this action" pursuant to district case law, on basis that Copyright Act's three-year statute of limitations had expired, so plaintiff could not re-file claim. However, court applied "discovery rule" to calculate statute of limitations and determined that plaintiff still had several years from date of discovery of infringement to re-file its claims, which were dismissed without prejudice. As statute of limitations had not run and plaintiff remained free to re-file claims, defendant not eligible for attorneys' fees as "prevailing party."

> *Stringer v. Richard*, No. 21-632, 2023 U.S. Dist. LEXIS 122818 (N.D. Ohio Jul. 17, 2023)

Plaintiff group of gospel music performers sued defendant gospel performer alleging defendant illegally used part of plaintiffs' copyrighted song "Abundance of Rain" (namely, refrain harmony "Let it fall on me") in defendant's song "Sauce." After district court granted summary judgment for defendant on infringement claims, defendant moved for attorneys' fees and costs. In ruling for defendant, district court held that plaintiffs "asserted frivolous and unreasonable legal positions, ignored fatal defects in their claims, and continued with the lawsuit to coerce Defendant to settle for a larger amount." Court found that plaintiffs brought sound recording copyright claim "despite not owning a sound recording copyright for the arguably copied song"—and even though defendant's counsel brought this defect to plaintiffs' attention early in dispute, plaintiffs persisted with litigation. Despite these defects, as well as lack of standing as to certain plaintiffs (who were not named in musical composition copyright), plaintiffs continued to pursue their sound recording copyright claim. District court held that plaintiff's "unreasonable behavior needs to be discouraged," and granted fees. Court did find that musical composition copyright claim (although ultimately defective because plaintiffs failed to establish that they independently created work) not objectively unreasonable, and thus reduced fees award by 20%. Applying lodestar method, district court found defendant's attorneys' hourly rates reasonable, and after applying 20% reduction granted defendant $81,168.80 in fees and costs.

Versluys v. Weizenbaum, No. 21-1694, 2024 U.S. Dist. LEXIS 38364 (D. Or. Mar. 4, 2024)

District court held defendants entitled to fees under Act. Plaintiffs alleged defendants taught seminars using PowerPoint slides that infringed copyrighted slides of plaintiffs. Court granted summary judgment for defendants, finding plaintiffs did not respond to defendants' argument that plaintiffs' expert report did not satisfy extrinsic test for purposes of proving copyright claim. Court determined plaintiffs' claim objectively unreasonable because rested on shaky evidence, at best. Plaintiffs' expert identified only 15 of defendants' slides that were allegedly substantially similar to plaintiffs' slides, and did not respond to defendants' arguments that slides contained different passages, translated passages differently, and used different diagrams. Court found plaintiffs sought to protect unprotectible ideas, as claim only applied to arrangement of content on slides and not ideas slides expressed. Court determined plaintiffs brought weak copyright claim against competitor, which suggested plaintiffs brought suit for reasons other than protecting copyrights, namely, to stifle competition, and defendants presented evidence to reinforce inference. Court found deterrence factor weighed in favor of defendants because plaintiffs had history of trying to stifle competition by threatening legal action and maligning reputation of competitors. Court determined awarding fees consistent with aims of Copyright Act to promote creative works that benefit public, especially works at issue based on ancient texts and practices widely available to public.

C. Injunction/Impoundment

Sibanda v. Elison, No. 23-5752, 2023 U.S. Dist. LEXIS 194629 (S.D.N.Y. Oct. 31, 2023)

District court denied plaintiff's motion for preliminary injunction. Plaintiff, lawyer proceeding *pro se*, alleged that 2019 movie *Gemini Man* infringed his copyright in book titled *The Return to Gibraltar*. Court noted party moving for preliminary injunction must establish irreparable harm and that preliminary injunction is in public interest, as well as either likelihood of success on merits or "sufficiently serious questions going to merits of its claims to make them fair ground for litigation, plus balance of hardships tipping decidedly in favor of moving party. Court did not need to consider latter factors because court found plaintiff failed to establish "single most important prerequisite" for preliminary injunctive relief, irreparable harm. Specifically, plaintiff failed to show or even claim book sales had suffered due to defendant's alleged infringement. Plaintiff asserted defendant's infringement jeopardized existence of plaintiff's creative licenses and derivative rights based on book, and harmed his goodwill and reputation. Court rejected such arguments, since allegedly infringing movie was already released, lawsuit primarily sought to prevent defendants from profiting unfairly, and plaintiff could be fully compensated by money damages in event that he prevails on his copyright claims. As such, plaintiff's motion for preliminary injunction was denied.

Tolkien Tr. v. Polychron, No. 23-4300, 2023 U.S. Dist. LEXIS 226135 (C.D. Cal. Dec. 14, 2023)

District court issued permanent injunction against defendant. Defendant Demetrious Polychron previously filed infringement and unfair competition claims against two Amazon companies, as well as entities and individual related to J.R.R. Tolkien estate. Polychron alleged Amazon and Tolkien estate had infringed his copyright in unauthorized derivative work *The Fellowship of the King* that was based on defendants' registered work. Amazon and Tolkien estate each filed motions to dismiss, which were granted. Subsequently, in present case, entities related to Tolkien estate filed infringement suit against Polychron, alleging that *The Fellowship of the King* infringed *The Lord of the Rings* by J.R.R. Tolkien. Tolkien plaintiffs moved for summary judgment and permanent injunction against Polychron. District court granted plaintiffs' motion for summary judgment. With respect to four factors for injunction analysis, district court held that (1) plaintiffs were likely to suffer irreparable harm because defendant might engage in infringement again, despite his contention he stopped selling infringing work; (2) plaintiffs did not have adequate remedy at law because they were likely to suffer irreparable harm if defendant continued to infringe; (3) balance of hardships tipped in plaintiffs' favor because injunction would cause little harm to defendant, who was already prohibited from infringing by Copyright

Act itself; and (4) public interest is served by protecting holder of valid copyright from infringement. Therefore, district court granted plaintiffs' request for permanent injunction against defendant's copying, distributing, and exploitation of defendant's work and any work by J.R.R. Tolkien—including but not limited to any derivative thereof.

NEO4J, Inc. v. Purethink, LLC, No. 18-7182, 2023 U.S. Dist. LEXIS 191809 (N.D. Cal. Oct. 25, 2023)

District court granted plaintiffs' motion for partial summary judgment. Plaintiffs, owner of graph database management systems and software and source code copyrights, sued defendant software developer for knowingly removing copyright management information within plaintiffs' software after receiving license to use plaintiffs' software. CMI was allegedly contained within plaintiffs' licensing terms and conditions and source code files. Defendants counterargued that plaintiffs had violated separate GNU Affero General Public License (AGPL) copyright license from non-party Free Software Foundation (FSF) governing content within plaintiffs' software, by modifying license; therefore, defendants argued, not only were defendants not engaging in knowing removal of CMI, but they were actually preventing further infringement by removing unauthorized terms from plaintiffs' software. District court rejected defendants' argument, because defendants are not owner of FSF's software copyrights and therefore cannot enforce such rights. In addition, court's prior summary judgment order had already decided substantially same issue; law of case thus prohibited defendants from raising it again. Furthermore, court re-affirmed that AGPL does not permit licensee to remove CMI from plaintiffs' license. District court granted plaintiffs' request for preliminary injunction against defendants, because plaintiffs established that (a) by removing commercial restrictions from plaintiff's software license, defendants convinced US government to download software for free instead of obtaining license from plaintiffs, thereby causing irreparable injury; (b) loss of control over software license cannot be compensated by monetary damages only; and (c) balance of hardships weighed in plaintiffs' favor, in part because defendants could not reasonably claim that prohibiting them from violating DMCA would impose hardship on them.

Sony Music Ent., Inc. v. Clark-Rainbolt, No. 23-275, 2024 U.S. Dist. LEXIS 54798 (N.D. Tex. Mar. 27, 2024)

District court permanently enjoined defendant from exploiting plaintiffs' copyrights without royalty payments. Plaintiffs, Sony record label and publisher, sued defendant for infringing composition and sound recording copyrights in Toshifumi Hinata's "Reflections" by impermissibly sampling it in defendant's song "90mh." Court granted judgment on pleadings in Sony's favor and parties submitted briefing concerning injunctive and monetary relief. In addition to award of defendant's revenues, to which court held Sony was entitled, Sony sought injunction permanently enjoining defendant from "copying, performing or otherwise exploiting '90mh' in any manner" and, if defendant failed to comply with injunction, order awarding Sony with 50% and 20% of revenues connected to defendant's composition and sound recording, respectively. Noting that injunction was extraordinary remedy requiring showing of irreparable harm, and in light of $800,000+ damages award, court denied Sony's injunction request. Instead, court enjoined defendant from exploiting "90mh" without paying 50% and 20% of revenues connected to his composition and sound recording, respectively, to Sony.

AFG Media Ltd. v. Poptrend-Official, No. 23-1840, 2023 U.S. Dist. LEXIS 230686 (W.D. Pa. Dec. 29, 2023)

Plaintiff seller of costumes owned copyright in design of alien costume with features that "give[] the viewer the impression that a person is being carried around by an alien." Plaintiff sued group of e-commerce sellers alleging infringement by selling knock-off alien costumes. After court issued temporary restraining order, plaintiff moved for preliminary injunction. Having found likelihood of success on merits, court considered remaining Third Circuit factors, namely: irreparable harm; that injunction will not result in even greater harm to non-moving party; and that public interest favors relief. On irreparable harm factor, defendants argued that plaintiff delayed in asserting its claim, and as such could not demonstrate irreparable harm; defendants also argued that plaintiff had adequate remedy available in form of statutory damages. Court rejected delay argument, finding that plaintiff timely filed lawsuit shortly after receiving actual knowledge of infringing conduct. Court similarly rejected argument that adequate remedy was available at law, finding defendants' conduct in selling substantially similar costumes caused market confusion and threatened plaintiff's "reputation, value, and goodwill" in manner that could not be adequately remedied at law. On balance of equities factor, defendants argued that ongoing freeze of its Amazon accounts had and would cause defendants irreparable harm, including loss of "significant portion of its revenue that is not relevant to its case." Although court found plaintiff ultimately likely to suffer greater hardship absent injunction, court did "narrow the injunctive relief" from enjoining all sales on defendants' online storefronts to enjoining only sales of alien costumes at issue in case. On public interest factor, court found public has interest in protection of intellectual property. Finding all factors favored plaintiff, court issued preliminary injunction.

Tecnoglass LLC v. Paredes, No. 22- 22356, 2023 U.S. Dist. LEXIS 116974 (S.D. Fla. July 6, 2023)

Plaintiff, manufacturer and owner of copyright in technical drawings relating to windows, sliding glass doors, and window wall systems for use in residential and construction industries, sued subcontractor for infringement, alleging defendant copied and used works as part of permit submissions for construction contracts. Plaintiff moved for summary judgment and permanent injunction, and having granted summary judgment on infringement, district court considered 11th Circuit permanent injunction factors, namely whether plaintiff demonstrated (1) success on merits; (2) irreparable injury for which monetary remedies are inadequate; (3) balance of hardships in favor of plaintiff; and (4) public interest would not be disserved by permanent injunction. On first factor, district court found plaintiff had succeeded on merits through its successful summary judgment motion on infringement. District court rejected defendants' argument that plaintiff failed to prove defendants' principal individually infringed, finding that individual defendant was person who conducted infringing activity on behalf of defendant entity, and thus plaintiff succeeded on merits as to all defendant parties. On second factor, district court found plaintiff stood to suffer irreparable harm, pointing to its prior findings on this point on previously-granted motion for preliminary injunction. On third factor, district court noted neither party addressed prong of permanent injunction test in their briefing, but likewise pointed to prior findings at preliminary injunction stage that threatened harm to plaintiff associated with suffering infringement outweighed any harm to defendants. On fourth factor, defendants failed to offer any rebuttal to plaintiff's argument that preliminary injunction would uphold copyright protection and prevent misappropriation of protected works. Preliminary injunction granted in favor of plaintiff.

cPanel, LLC v. Asli, No. 22-1963, 2024 U.S. Dist. LEXIS 1746 (D. Or. Jan. 3, 2024)

District court granted motion for preliminary injunction against alleged cybersquatter. Plaintiff developed software providing users with graphical interface and tools for managing and hosting websites, and sold licenses for use of software. Defendants allegedly sold illicit licenses to plaintiff's software on websites bearing domain names incorporating name of plaintiff's software. Defendant also changed lines of software's code in unsuccessful attempt to make their use undetectable by plaintiff. Court found that plaintiff showed likelihood of success on merits on claims of copyright infringement and trafficking of circumvention devices in violation of DMCA due to defendant's alteration of software to avoid detection. Court found harm to be irreparable despite defendant's voluntarily making websites inaccessible, because there was nothing preventing defendant from making sites available again.

Nat'l Presto Indus. v. United States Merchs. Fin. Grp., Inc., No. 18-3321, 2023 U.S. Dist. LEXIS 206092 (D. Minn. Nov. 17, 2023)

Court denied plaintiff's motion for permanent injunction. Plaintiff Presto manufactured electric heater called HeatDish and sold it exclusively to Costco. In 2017, Costco sought new heater supplier. Defendant U.S. Merchants contacted suppliers and obtained samples of plaintiff's HeatDish and by late 2017, developed its own heater, The Heat Machine, and sold to Costco. Original manual for The Heat Machine had similar language to plaintiff's 1995 HeatDish manual. After plaintiff sued for copyright infringement in December 2018, defendant continued selling heaters with original manual for several more weeks before revising it. Following jury trial, plaintiff awarded $150,000 in statutory damages for defendant's copyright infringement. Plaintiff sought permanent injunction protecting its copyright in 1995 manual from further infringement. Court denied request. Defendant had not distributed at-issue manual for several years and was distributing new iterations of its heaters with revised manual since 2019. Plaintiff raised specter of future infringement, but never claimed infringement with respect to defendant's more recent manuals. Further, parties agreed, and jury found, no actual damages for defendant's infringement of plaintiff's copyright in 1995 manual. Plaintiff's claim for real harm in future—let alone irreparable harm—speculative.

Elgin Separation Sols., LLC v. Dillon, No. 23-440, 2023 U.S. Dist. LEXIS 184499 (S.D. W. Va. Oct. 13, 2023)

District court denied plaintiffs' motion for preliminary injunction. Plaintiffs and defendants both provided services and goods related to repair and manufacture of decanter centrifuges, mechanical devices that separate solids from slurries (for example, in coal mining). Defendant Chad Dillon sold his decanter centrifuge business to Elgin, but years later left to start his own competing business once his non-competition restrictions expired. Prior to leaving Elgin, Dillon forwarded to himself copy of manual that Elgin had prepared for customer. Elgin later registered copyright in manual and sued defendants for infringement. Elgin's copyright was not registered within three months of publication or prior to commencement of infringement, thereby precluding statutory damages and attorneys' fees. District court concluded Elgin had not demonstrated likelihood of irreparable harm with respect to copyright claim, because evidence presented did not indicate that defendants used or intended to use subject work in competition with Elgin. District court therefore denied plaintiffs' motion for preliminary injunction.

VIII. PREEMPTION

Best Carpet Values, Inc. v. Google, LLC, 90 F.4th 962 (9th Cir. 2024)

Ninth Circuit reversed denial of Google's motion to dismiss class action. Plaintiffs challenged Google's method of displaying websites in Search App on Android phones, arguing that by including option to display large previews of competitors' similar sites onscreen when users visit plaintiffs' sites, Google trespassed on their chattels. After finding that trespass on chattels claim should be dismissed because plaintiffs had no property interest in how copies of their websites are shown, Ninth Circuit also found that district court should have dismissed plaintiffs' "implied-in-law contract and unjust enrichment" claim as preempted by Copyright Act. This claim also argued that plaintiffs have property interest in how their sites are shown, but Ninth Circuit found that how websites are displayed on user's screen falls within subject matter of copyright law, and rights asserted by plaintiffs were equivalent to rights provided by copyright law. Plaintiffs could not identify how covering part of their sites for financial benefit was different from claim for unauthorized derivative work. Even if plaintiffs' claim were instead framed as allegation that Google exceeded scope of its license to reproduce copies of websites, this fails because plaintiffs could not identify what scope of alleged license was and how Google exceeded that scope.

Neu Productions Inc. v. Outside Interactive, Inc., No. 23-4125, 2024 U.S. Dist. LEXIS 47842 (S.D.N.Y. Mar. 19, 2024)

District court granted motion to dismiss common law claims based on licensing agreement as preempted. Plaintiff film production company created programs for defendant, operator of outdoors-themed television channels and streaming services. Plaintiffs filmed 16 episodes of television series and licensed them to defendant for use on its television channel for limited time pursuant to what parties agreed was implied license. Plaintiffs licensed additional show to defendant in perpetuity. Plaintiffs alleged that defendant expanded its use of plaintiffs' content beyond defendant's television channel and onto defendants' streaming service, exceeding scope of parties' agreements. Plaintiffs filed infringement claim against defendant's expanded use and also brought claims for breach of contract, unjust enrichment, and misappropriation of right of publicity. Court dismissed all those claims as preempted. Breach of contract claim and unjust enrichment claims were both based on defendant allegedly exceeding license agreement, which was already subject of plaintiffs' claim under Copyright Act. One individual plaintiff—host of program at issue—brought separate unjust enrichment and right of publicity claims based on defendant's unauthorized use of his celebrity status, name, voice, and image beyond scope of his quasi-contractual agreement with defendant, but these too were covered by Copyright Act, as they dealt with that plaintiff's efforts to control copying, distribution, and public performance of works at issue.

Gordon v. Kaiser Found. Health Plan, Inc., No. 23-1507, 2023 U.S. Dist. LEXIS 223921 (S.D. Cal. Dec. 15, 2023)

District court partially dismissed plaintiff's claims based on preemption and remanded remaining claims to state court. Plaintiff Nancy M. Gordon, author of self-help books based on personal traumatic experiences, wrote 7 STEPS of HOPE workbook in approximately October 2014, and subsequently shared it with defendant physical therapists at defendant Kaiser Foundation Health Plan while she was receiving treatment. Plaintiff agreed to sell her workbook to defendants, who signed NDA. Plaintiff later changed her mind and rescinded sale; defendant asked plaintiff to destroy NDA and claimed that none of plaintiff's information was disclosed. Several years later, plaintiff returned to Kaiser and discovered that Kaiser's pain program was allegedly substantially similar to plaintiff's original work. Plaintiff asserted nine causes of action, including breach of implied contract, fraud and intentional and negligent misrepresentation, intentional and negligent infliction of emotional distress, negligence, violations of California's Business and Professions Code, and civil conspiracy. Defendants removed case to federal court based on federal question jurisdiction; defendant then filed motion to dismiss based on preemption. Plaintiff filed motion to remand. Using two-factor test for preemption, district court first concluded that plaintiff's allegations were based on defendants' use of plaintiff's system, process, or ideas that were "fixed" in her subject work and therefore fell within subject matter of copyright. Regarding second prong, district court found that breach of implied contract, quasi-contract, fraud and intentional and negligent misrepresentation, business and professions code, and civil conspiracy claims were not preempted. However, intentional and negligent infliction of emotional distress and negligence claims were preempted, because conduct regarding alleged distress was rooted in defendants' unauthorized use of subject work, and negligence claim was based in part on defendants' improper use of content of subject work. District court therefore dismissed emotional distress and negligence claims due to preemption, declined to exercise supplemental jurisdiction over remaining claims, and remanded them to California Superior Court.

Laatz v. Zazzle, Inc., 682 F. Supp. 3d 791 (N.D. Cal. 2023)

Court denied defendants' motion to dismiss. Plaintiff created fonts and licensed use of font and relevant software. Defendant Zazzle, Inc. maintained site where consumers could create and/or purchase customizable products. Plaintiff alleged that Zazzle employee contacted plaintiff to ask about perpetual license for font for use on internal server and for customization tool. Because plaintiff did not enter into server-based license for font and font software, plaintiff did not respond. Months later, Zazzle employee purchased license for Plaintiff's font software and agreed to terms of use for license to individual. Plaintiff alleged that individual employee then downloaded font and software and copied both onto Zazzle servers, after which Zazzle integrated font and software into its customization tool, making font available to millions to use, including for commercial use. Plaintiff filed suit, and defendants moved to dismiss on grounds that complaint failed to state claim for infringement and Act preempted state law claims. As to merits of infringement claim, court began analysis by noting that typeface was not protectable by itself, but that font software was copyrightable. Although plaintiff used FontLab to create code, complaint sufficiently pleaded that plaintiff "hand-coded" aspects of code. While court acknowledged "serious questions" as to sufficiency of plaintiff's contributions to be considered author, it found question inappropriate on motion to dismiss. Plaintiff additionally sufficiently alleged infringement. As to preemption arguments, court assessed fraud-based and breach of contract claims separately. Court found fraud claims not preempted because misrepresentation occurring prior to infringement amounted to pleaded extra element. On contract claim, court found contract contained different rights than those in Act, such as allowing for use by single user on two computers. Court denied motion to dismiss.

> *Bold Ltd. v. Rocket Resume, Inc.*, No. 22-1045, 2023 U.S. Dist. LEXIS 108212 (N.D. Cal. June 22, 2023)

District court denied motion to dismiss because breach of contract claim not preempted. Plaintiff owned and operated MyPerfectResume website, interactive website allowing users to create resume, including by using lists of prewritten job descriptions. MPR's terms of use required users to agree not to share or use data mining software to collect content from MPR website. Plaintiff discovered that defendant had created competing website containing so many identical job descriptions that plaintiff believed defendant had stolen information from MPR website using automated means. Plaintiff sued for, *inter alia*, breach of contract based on terms of use. Court held that claim not preempted because prohibition of use of certain software in connection with website related to actions other than copying and reproduction of copyrighted content.

> *HCL Techs. Ltd. v. Atos S.E.*, No. 23-868, 2024 U.S. Dist. LEXIS 44038 (N.D. Tex. Mar. 12, 2024)

District court overruled both parties' objections to magistrate's recommended dismissal of unjust enrichment claim as against only one set of defendants. Plaintiffs sued two sets of defendants, Atos Defendants and CNA Defendants, for using plaintiffs' computer software in violation of parties' licenses. Plaintiffs did not have business relationship with CNA Defendants, only with Atos Defendants. Magistrate found that plaintiffs' unjust enrichment claim as to CNA Defendants was preempted by copyright law, but was not as to Atos Defendants because, viewing facts in light most favorable to plaintiffs, Atos Defendants took "undue advantage" of business relationship with plaintiffs when they continued using plaintiffs' software after licensing agreement expired. As such, additional element found in unjust enrichment claim as to Atos Defendants and it was not equivalent to exclusive copyright rights.

> *Uworld LLC v. Usmle Galaxy LLC*, No. 23-447, 2023 U.S. Dist. LEXIS 119673 (N.D. Tex. June 27, 2023)

District court held that plaintiff's state law claims under Texas Theft Liability Act and Texas Unfair competition Law were preempted. Plaintiff, nursing exam test preparation company, sued competitor company alleging that it had infringed copyrighted bank of practice questions and test preparation materials, thereby violating Texas Theft Liability Act, Texas Unfair Competition Act and Federal Copyright law. Court granted defendants' motion to dismiss Texas Theft Liability

Act and Texas Unfair Competition Law claims as preempted since claims were based on allegations of infringing copyrightable materials.

Eggleston v. Twentieth Century Fox Film Corp., No. 21-11171, 2023 U.S. Dist. LEXIS 176139 (E.D. Mich. Sept. 29, 2023)

District court granted defendant's motion to dismiss plaintiff's state unjust enrichment claim as preempted. Plaintiff had previously sued defendants in 2015 for copyright infringement, arguing that character of Cookie Lyon on defendants' TV show *Empire* was based on plaintiff's life as portrayed in her memoir *The Hidden Hand.* Previous suit was dismissed voluntarily without prejudice when plaintiff's competency was called into question in contemporaneous criminal case. In 2021, plaintiff filed new suit renewing copyright infringement claim but, when defendants moved to dismiss, plaintiff amended complaint to expressly disavow any copyright infringement claim and instead raised single claim for unjust enrichment under Michigan law. Plaintiff alleged that, in 2011, *Empire*'s screenwriter had interviewed her about her life story and received copy of plaintiff's memoir. Court held that, despite plaintiff's argument that she sought compensation solely for her labor in developing Cookie Lyon character (i.e., time spent with screenwriter rather than specific copyrighted material from memoir), those intangible-concept based contributions cannot be separated from tangible expressions in copyrighted memoir. Because plaintiff's unjust enrichment claim was nothing more than relabeled, previously-dismissed copyright infringement claim, former was preempted.

Design Gaps, Inc. v. Hall, No. 23-186, 2023 U.S. Dist. LEXIS 208773 (W.D.N.C. Nov. 21, 2023)

District court granted defendants' motion to dismiss plaintiffs' claims under Lanham Act and Unfair and Deceptive Trade Practice Act ("UDTPA") on basis that claims were preempted by Copyright Act. Plaintiffs alleged defendants copied plaintiffs' interior cabinetry designs for homes and marketed designs as defendants' own works, and that such conduct constituted false designation of origin and false advertising in violation of Lanham Act and UDTPA. Court applied two-prong test to determine whether claims preempted by Copyright Act: claim is preempted if (1) work is within subject matter of copyright and (2) claim seeks to vindicate rights equivalent to those protected by copyright law. Court also noted that claim may be preempted even if subject matter of work could not be registered with Copyright Office. In finding preemption, court noted plaintiffs' complaint referred to designs as "copyrights" in multiple instances; plaintiffs used "terms synonymous with 'copyright' throughout the Amended Complaint"; and plaintiffs recently filed separate federal action asserting copyright registrations for designs. Court agreed with defendants that designs "fit within the general subject matter exclusively earmarked … for copyright protection" and found plaintiffs did not include "extra element[s]" to distinguish claims from copyright claims.

As such, court found slaims satisfied second prong of preemption test as claims sought to vindicate rights equivalent to those protected by copyright law. Court dismissed claims as preempted by Copyright Act.

IX. DIGITAL MILLENNIUM COPYRIGHT ACT

Loeb-Defever v. Mako, LLC, No. 22-20362, 2023 U.S. App. LEXIS 23004 (5th Cir. Aug. 30, 2023)

Circuit court affirmed district court's grant of summary judgment to defendants on infringement and DMCA claims. Plaintiff, architect, sued defendants, developers for senior living facility, for infringement and violations of DMCA for allegedly using plaintiff's copyrighted schematics to develop facility. Plaintiffs granted defendants express, nonexclusive license to use preliminary design in connection with project. Parties argued over scope of license. Court found contract granted defendants license to use schematics to create derivative works because gave right to reproduce, and provisions suggested discretion to distribute and use schematics throughout project. Court determined contract title and relevant provisions established parties intended schematics to be used both for financing purposes and as conceptual springboard for later design stages. Court found contract allowed for express authorization of defendant to use third parties to implement license. Court held defendants' use of preliminary design schematics to create derivative works and subsequent marketing, rental, and sale of facilities did not exceed scope of license. Court held plaintiff failed to establish genuine dispute of DMCA claim because defendants could not have intended or known conduct would induce, enable, facilitate, or conceal infringement when they were not infringing copyright because they held license.

We the Protesters, Inc. v. Sinyangwe, No. 22-9565, 2024 U.S. Dist. LEXIS 49532 (S.D.N.Y. Mar. 20, 2024)

District court denied plaintiffs' motion to dismiss infringement counterclaim, finding defendants properly alleged ownership of valid copyright and copying of constituent elements of work that are original, and granted plaintiffs' motion to dismiss DMCA counterclaim only as to modified website. Defendants created website that collected and assembled information on reported incidents of police violence across country. Plaintiffs entered into collaboration with defendants. Defendants alleged that plaintiffs attempted to gain access to defendants' account to access or edit website, and after failed attempt, published copycat version of website. Court determined defendants did not need to assert exactly which individual elements of copyrighted works were infringed at motion to dismiss stage. Court found concept of websites, mapping incidents of police killings, undoubtedly similar, but had doubts over proposition that protectible aspects of website were substantially similar to those in plaintiffs'. Court found plaintiffs' arguments attacking defendants' selection, coordination, and arrangement theory unavailing because fact that plaintiffs were unable to accurately update database allegedly copied does not mean plaintiffs did not copy database in first instance. Court also found unavailing plaintiff's argument that police killings data constituted basic facts not copyrightable because argument failed to take into account that defendants' copyright claim concerned selection, coordination, and arrangement of those facts and not facts themselves. Court found website passed originality test because defendants used color choices and picked certain graphics with specific goal in mind. Plaintiffs also moved to dismiss DMCA counterclaim which alleges plaintiffs violated DMCA's prohibition on removing CMI from website. Court granted plaintiffs' motion to dismiss counterclaim inasmuch as claim was predicated on plaintiffs' modified website because website and plaintiffs' modified website distinct. However, website and plaintiffs' original website were at least close to identical so court at motion to dismiss stage allowed counterclaim to proceed only on basis of pre-modified version of website.

Lane Coder Photography, LLC v. Hearst Corp., No. 22-5071, 2023 U.S. Dist. LEXIS 159200 (S.D.N.Y. Sept. 8, 2023)

District court granted defendant Hearst's motion to dismiss plaintiff professional photographer's DMCA claim where plaintiff had not plausibly pleaded existence of any CMI on original photos and failed to explain how defendant would have had access to it. Plaintiff was commissioned by Sotheby's to photograph Connecticut real estate "Greenacre." Pursuant to parties' agreement, Sotheby was to use photos for advertising property's sale and could not sub-license photos or transmit to other parties. Plaintiff obtained group copyright registration of photos. Shortly after, defendant Hearst Corporation published two online articles using several of plaintiff's photos without plaintiff's authorization—some with attribution to Sotheby's, some without. Plaintiff did not authorize display or use of photos, which he claims featured copyright management information when provided to Sotheby's. Plaintiff alleges defendant Hearst obtained photos from Sotheby's website and removed plaintiff's CMI. Defendant Hearst moved to dismiss plaintiff's DMCA claim. Court concluded plaintiff's claims must fail, as plaintiff had not sufficiently allege threshold element of CMI removal or alteration claim—that original infringed work featured any CMI. Here, plaintiff's complaint alleged in conclusory fashion that he transmitted photos to Sotheby's with CMI, including authorship and ownership credits. Complaint failed to include exhibits showing original photos or their CMI, nor did plaintiff include description of what original CMI looked like, where it appeared, or by what method he transmitted photos. As such, court was unable to discern whether defendant altered or removed CMI when it reproduced photos. DMCA claims were dismissed without prejudice.

Tremblay v. OpenAI, Inc., Nos. 23-3223; 23-3416, 2024 U.S. Dist. LEXIS 24618 (N.D. Cal. Feb. 12, 2024)

District court dismissed plaintiffs' DMCA claims for intentional removal or alteration of CMI and distribution of works or copies. Plaintiffs, authors of books who alleged that their books were used to train OpenAI language models operating ChatGPT, sued defendant OpenAI, creator and seller of large language model AI software. Plaintiffs alleged direct and vicarious infringement and DMCA claims. OpenAI copied plaintiffs' copyrighted books and used them in its training dataset. When prompted to summarize books written by each plaintiff, ChatGPT generated accurate summaries. Plaintiffs sought to represent class of all people in U.S. who owned copyright in any work that was used in training data for OpenAI language models. OpenAI moved to dismiss certain claims, including DMCA claims. Plaintiffs' complaint included DMCA claims under two subsections. Court first found plaintiffs failed to allege facts to show defendant unlawfully removed plaintiffs' copyright management information from copyrighted books used during training process. In fact, outputs sometimes did reference plaintiffs, indicating it did not remove names of authors. Similarly, plaintiffs made only conclusory allegations that "by design, the training process does not preserve any CMI." Even if plaintiffs had provided facts showing defendant's knowing removal of CMI from books during training, plaintiffs have not shown how omitting CMI in copies used in training gave defendant reasonable grounds to know ChatGPT's output would induce, enable, facilitate, or conceal infringement—knowledge requirement under DMCA statute. Second claim dealt with statute subsection requiring distribution of original "works" or "copies of works" for liability. Plaintiffs did not allege defendant distributed their books or copies of books. Instead, they alleged that every output from OpenAI language models is infringing derivative work without providing indication as to what such outputs entail. Plaintiffs' arguments insufficient to support this cause of action under DMCA. Both DMCA claims were dismissed.

NEO4J, Inc. v. Purethink, LLC, No. 18-7182, 2023 U.S. Dist. LEXIS 191809 (N.D. Cal. Oct. 25, 2023)

District court granted plaintiffs' motion for partial summary judgment. Plaintiffs, owner of graph database management systems and software and source code copyrights, sued defendant software developer for knowingly removing copyright management information within plaintiffs' software after receiving license to use plaintiffs' software. CMI was allegedly contained within plaintiffs' licensing terms and conditions and source code files. Defendants counterargued that plaintiffs had violated separate GNU Affero General Public License ("AGPL") copyright license from non-party Free Software Foundation ("FSF") governing content within plaintiffs' software, by modifying license; therefore, defendants argued, not only were defendants not engaging in knowing removal of CMI, but they were actually preventing further infringement, by removing unauthorized terms from plaintiffs' software. District court rejected defendants' argument, because defendants were not owners of FSF's software copyrights and therefore could not enforce such rights. In addition, court's prior summary judgment order had already decided substantially same issue; law of case thus prohibited defendants from raising it again. Furthermore, court re-affirmed that AGPL does not permit licensee to remove CMI from plaintiffs' license. District court granted plaintiffs' request for preliminary injunction against defendants, because plaintiffs established that (a) by removing commercial restrictions from plaintiff's software license, defendants had convinced U.S. government to download software for free instead of obtaining license from plaintiffs, thereby causing irreparable injury; (b) loss of control over software license cannot be compensated by monetary damages only; and (c) balance of hardships weighed in plaintiffs' favor, in part because defendants could not reasonably claim that prohibiting them from violating DMCA would impose hardship on them.

Shande v. Zoox, Inc., No. 22-5821, 2023 U.S. Dist. LEXIS 141606 (N.D. Cal. Aug. 14, 2023)

District court dismissed infringement claim brought by copyright owner against defendant who issued successful DMCA takedown notice against plaintiff's work, which was similar to work made by plaintiff when employed by defendant. Plaintiff was employed by defendant autonomous vehicle company to create digital street scenery of San Francisco. Plaintiff also created what he said was unrelated digital street scenery of San Francisco that he sold on online marketplace operated by non-party Epic Games. Defendant submitted DMCA takedown notice to Epic that resulted in removal of content. Plaintiff sued defendant for knowing misrepresentation under DMCA, infringement of exclusive copyright interest, and state claims. Court granted motion to dismiss DMCA claim with leave to amend, as plaintiff's claim did not clearly assert that defendant acted with subjective bad faith when sending takedown notice to Epic. Court also dismissed copyright infringement claim, finding that asserting ownership of content in DMCA claim is not usurpation of plaintiff's right to distribute copies of his work.

Fashion Nova, LLC v. Blush Mark, Inc., No. 22-6127, 2023 U.S. Dist. LEXIS 114601 (C.D. Cal. June 30, 2023)

District court granted defendants' motion to dismiss without leave to amend. Plaintiff alleged defendants willfully infringed copyrights in various product images displayed on plaintiff's website and removed/altered images' CMI in violation of DMCA. Court found plaintiff's file names did not constitute CMI based on author name because plaintiff failed to specify how file names identified authors, and file name alone did not clearly notify viewer that images were copyrighted. Further, even if file names contained words or letters that referred to author, plaintiff did not explain how they matched information in copyright registrations. Court also found plaintiff failed to identify how file names that included numbers and symbols identified work as copyrighted. Court similarly found product names alone not to constitute CMI because they did not reveal to viewer that images were copyrighted. Court found amendment would be futile and denied leave to amend.

Roadget Bus. PTE. LTD v. PDD Holdings Inc., No. 22-07119, 2023 U.S. Dist. LEXIS 131974 (N.D. Ill. July 31, 2023)

District court granted plaintiff's request for emergency temporary restraining order because court found plaintiff showed likelihood of success on copyright infringement claims and defendant did not qualify for DMCA safe harbor provision. Plaintiff, owner of registrations associated with Shein, online fashion and lifestyle retailer, sued defendant, owner of mobile application and website, for infringement. Court found that plaintiff established unauthorized copying, and that defendant exercised more control over third-party sellers and products sold on its platforms than similar digital marketplaces. Plaintiff produced evidence from defendant's own website and communications as well as articles detailing defendant's full-service model to defeat defendant's DMCA safe harbor arguments, and defendant did not provide rebutting evidence.

Trent P. Fisher Enters., LLC v. SAS Automation, LLC, No. 20-216, 2023 U.S. Dist. LEXIS 135933 (S.D. Ohio Aug. 3, 2023)

District court denied defendants' motion for summary judgment on plaintiffs' claim that defendant wrongfully removed copyright management information from plaintiffs' works. Plaintiffs sold defendant SAS to defendants Piab USA, Inc. and Piab AB. As part of transaction, plaintiffs transferred equity in SAS to Piab, but Piab assigned IP rights in SAS's proprietary e-commerce software ("Works") to plaintiffs to be licensed back to Piab. Works were developed in significant part with code from open-source e-commerce software OpenCart pursuant to GNU General Public License ("GPL"), obliging developers to publicly disclose source code and make work available for free use if software developed via GPL is "covered work" and "conveyed" to third party. When Piab developed in-house e-commerce software largely based on source code from Works, plaintiff sued for infringement, and alleged wrongful removal or alteration of CMI from Works pursuant to DMCA. In denying defendants' motion for summary judgment, court found that genuine issues of material fact remained as to questions of infringement related to whether GPL precludes infringement finding; if defendants were found to have infringed Works, plaintiffs would be allowed to prove damages based on removal of CMI.

Campbell v. Gannett Co., No. 21-557, 2023 U.S. Dist. LEXIS 142188 (W.D. Mo. Aug. 15, 2023)

District court granted defendants' summary judgment motions based on removal of copyright management information. Plaintiff sued defendants for removal of copyright management information in connection with plaintiff's photograph of National Football League (NFL) Coach Katie Sowers. Pursuant to license agreement, photo of Sowers was used in Microsoft ad entitled "Be The One" that aired during Super Bowl Commercial in 2020. Screenshot of plaintiff's photo was displayed on websites owned by defendants in connection with "Ad Meter" public survey regarding Super Bowl commercials. Plaintiff alleged that defendants had knowingly removed CMI, including plaintiff's name, from subject work. In response to defendants' summary judgment motion, plaintiff attempted to expand complaint's allegations, by claiming subject work contained Microsoft's name as owner of work, and alleging that defendants removed CMI without permission of Microsoft or plaintiff. District court rejected plaintiff's allegations not contained within complaint, and further held that plaintiff failed to present proof of removal of her CMI, as it was undisputed that plaintiff's CMI did not appear on or near original ad or still photograph within ad from which defendants took screengrab for their Ad Meter survey. District court accordingly granted defendant's motion for summary judgment on plaintiff's CMI claim.

VidAngel LLC v. ClearPlay, Inc., No. 14-160, 2023 U.S. Dist. LEXIS 207970 (D. Utah Nov. 20, 2023)

District court granted plaintiff's summary judgment motion dismissing defendant's DMCA counterclaim because no dispute of material fact that defendant was not copyright owner or supplier of technological control measure, or in privy with same, so not in zone of interests of DMCA. Both plaintiff and defendant offered products designed to remove objectionable content from multimedia. Plaintiff asserted defendant infringed patents and defendant counterclaimed plaintiff violated DMCA. Plaintiff argued defendant fell outside zone of interests of DMCA. Court found zone of interest language of DMCA includes copyright owners and owners of access control measures, but does not extend to those who allege competitive disadvantage flowing from alleged violation of copyrights or circumvention of access control measures with no legal interest. Court held defendant did not fall in zone of interest because defendant did not claim it owned copyrighted material plaintiff allegedly infringed, nor did it claim copyright owner authorized to protect copyrighted material. Defendant also did not claim it supplied any access control technology that plaintiff circumvented, nor did it allege it was agent or otherwise privy with such entity. Court found Congress did not intend for anyone seeking to enforce statute to fall within zone of interest. Court determined plaintiff entitled to judgment on defendant's DMCA claim.

Dermansky v. Hayride Media, LLC, No. 22-3491, 2023 U.S. Dist. LEXIS 168076 (E.D. La. Sept. 21, 2023)

District court granted plaintiff's motion for partial summary judgment and denied defendant's motion for summary judgment, holding that fair use defense failed as matter of law. Plaintiff Julie Dermansky, professional photographer, alleged that defendant Hayride, which operates conservative news blog and website, used plaintiff's photos of St. Tammany, Louisiana councilman speaking to anti-fracking protestors and of Baton Rouge community activist standing in front of flood-damaged belongings without approval, without paying licensing fee, and without crediting plaintiff. Defendant sought dismissal of infringement claims based on fair use defense. Regarding first fair use factor, defendant derived direct commercial benefit from use of subject works, and use was not transformative. Referencing recent Supreme Court *Warhol v. Goldsmith* decision, district court noted that use was not transformative because both plaintiff and defendants used photos as illustrative images for online news articles. Factual dispute regarding whether defendant lacked good faith in its use of images of photos was immaterial, because defendant failed to prove transformative use. Regarding second factor, plaintiff made "deliberate and intentional creative choices" that made works creative in nature, not just informational. Regarding third factor, defendant used substantial portion of works, because its purpose in using works was similar to plaintiff's, i.e., to illustrate news articles. Regarding fourth factor, defendant's use of plaintiff's works was deemed to be market substitute for original works, even though plaintiff and defendant had opposing political viewpoints. All four factors therefore weighed against fair use. Court accordingly denied defendant's motion for summary judgment and granted plaintiff's cross-motion.

X. VISUAL ARTISTS RIGHTS ACT

Kerson v. Vermont Law School, 79 F.4th 257 (2d Cir. 2023)

In 1993, plaintiff and Vermont Law School entered into agreement for plaintiff to paint two murals, rendered directly onto drywall of Community Center. First panel, entitled Slavery, included four scenes depicting (1) capture of people in Africa; (2) their sale in United States; (3) slave labor; and (4) slave insurrection. Second panel, entitled Liberation, portrayed (1) Harriet Beecher Stowe, John Brown, and Frederick Douglass; (2) Harriet Tubman arriving in Vermont; (3) residents of South Royalton, Vermont sheltering refugee slaves; and (4) Vermonters assisting escaped slaves. Murals proved controversial, and in 2014 Law School installed plaques beside Murals to explain their "intent to depict shameful history of slavery as well as Vermont's role in Underground Railway." In 2020 Law School received petition demanding removal of Murals. On learning of limitations imposed by VARA, Law School sent letter to plaintiff advising him that unless he arranged to remove work within 90 days, Law School would "proceed to remove or cover mural as it deems appropriate." Plaintiff arranged for Murals to be inspected by carpenters, who advised him that Murals could not be separated from drywall without being disfigured. Law School installed temporary cloth curtain to conceal Murals, and ultimately settled on concealing Murals behind barrier of fabric-cushioned acoustic panels. Plaintiff sued Law

School, seeking preliminary injunction enjoining it from placing panels over Murals, invoking his rights under VARA to prevent "destruction" or "intentional distortion, mutilation, or other modification" of Murals. District court denied plaintiff's motion for preliminary injunction and granted summary judgment to Law School, holding that VARA does not prohibit permanent concealment of work of visual art, absent any physical change to work itself. Court reasoned that "we do not frequently use 'modify' to describe moving object to location where it cannot be seen." Court was similarly unmoved by plaintiff's argument that Law School "threatened to modify" Murals by concealing them behind acoustic panels that over time could create environmental conditions that might damage Murals. Finally, based on "conventional definition of destruction," which "connotes obliteration and total loss," court rejected plaintiff's contention that hiding Murals behind barrier or possibly exposing them to deleterious environmental conditions was tantamount to destroying them. On appeal, plaintiff argued that district court adopted overly narrow construction of rights VARA confers upon artists. In plaintiff's view, wall of acoustic panels implicates VARA's protection because permanently concealing immovable artwork not only "modifies" it, but also "destroys" it for all intents and purposes. In addition, plaintiff sought to prevent Law School from exposing Murals to "potentially toxic environment" behind panels, which, he argued, could also result in Murals' destruction. Second Circuit affirmed, agreeing with district court that Law School neither "modified" nor "destroyed" Murals. Court found that plaintiff's reading did not comport with any conventional understanding of word "destruction." There was no dispute that Murals remained fully intact; panel wall was designed so as to not touch Murals, and thus did not physically alter them, let alone destroy them. Plaintiff also urged "more capacious" reading of "modification," arguing that term "is not limited to physical changes of the artwork itself, but rather includes changes in how the artwork is presented." Court disagreed, concluding that "modification" under VARA does not encompass concealing artwork from view in manner that does not otherwise alter work. Court further rejected plaintiff's contention that permitting Law School to conceal Murals was contrary to protection VARA affords to works that are "incorporated in or made part of building in such way that removing work from building will cause destruction, distortion, mutilation, or other modification of work." Plaintiff, Second Circuit found, "overread" relevant provisions, which merely specify circumstances in which owner may remove incorporated work from building into which it is incorporated, despite harm that will befall work as result. Here Law School had not removed Murals from Community Center; Murals remained intact and incorporated into building. Law School remained barred from intentionally or grossly negligently destroying Murals, and from modifying them so as to prejudice plaintiff's honor or reputation; but Law School neither modified nor destroyed Murals by concealing them behind wall of acoustic panels—and that result was no different because Murals were incorporated into building. Finally, court rejected plaintiff's claim, based on expert testimony, that acoustic panels would expose Murals to toxic environmental conditions that could damage them to point of distortion, mutilation, modification, or even destruction. Expert admitted that she had no knowledge of panels' composition, but opined nevertheless that acoustic panels were more likely than not to create ambient conditions that would damage Murals. Court held that, even accepting plaintiff's evidence that wall of panels might conceivably damage Murals at some undefined point in future, VARA prohibits only "intentional distortion, mutilation, or other modification" of works of visual art. And record was devoid of evidence that Law School, in placing panels in front of Murals, intended to harm or otherwise modify them. Court concluded on conciliatory note: "That said, nothing in our decision today precludes the parties from identifying a way to extricate the Murals from the Chase Community Center so as to preserve them as objects of art in a manner agreeable to all."

Cowan, Liebowitz & Latman Attorneys

Daniel Basov	**(212) 790-9278**	***dyb@cll.com***
Jeremy A. Bernman	**(212) 790-9293**	***jab@cll.com***
William M. Borchard	**(212) 790-9290**	***wmb@cll.com***
Jeffery Chery	**(212) 790-9263**	***jyc@cll.com***
Dasha Chestukhin	**(212) 790-9251**	***dxc@cll.com***
Richard Dannay	**(212) 790-9256**	***rxd@cll.com***
Mary A. Donovan	**(212) 790-9277**	***mad@cll.com***
Kieran G. Doyle	**(212) 790-9261**	***kgd@cll.com***
Robert J. English	**(212) 790-9215**	***rje@cll.com***
C. J. Erickson	**(212) 790-9274**	***cje@cll.com***
Lynn S. Fruchter	**(212) 790-9207**	***lsf@cll.com***
Allison R. Furnari	**(212) 790-9209**	***arf@cll.com***
Paige A. Geier	**(212) 790-9264**	***pag@cll.com***
Simon Gerson	**(212) 790-9206**	***sxg@cll.com***
Robert J. Giordanella	**(212) 790-9234**	***rjg@cll.com***
Kyle-Beth Hilfer	**(212) 790-9200**	***kbh@cll.com***
J. Christopher Jensen	**(212) 790-9204**	***jcj@cll.com***
Justin I. Karasick	**(212) 790-9272**	***jik@cll.com***
Mary L. Kelvin	**(212) 790-9216**	***mlk@cll.com***
Jonathan Z. King	**(212) 790-9238**	***jzk@cll.com***
Thomas Kielberg	**(212) 790-9202**	***txk@cll.com***
Sarah Sue Landau	**(212) 790-9246**	***ssl@cll.com***
Maryann Licciardi	**(212) 790-9218**	***mel@cll.com***
Meichelle R. MacGregor	**(212) 790-9259**	***mrm@cll.com***
Richard S. Mandel	**(212) 790-9221**	***rsm@cll.com***
Joelle A. Milov	**(212) 790-9247**	***jam@cll.com***
John S. Miranda	**(212) 790-9243**	***jsm@cll.com***
Mark Montague	**(212) 790-9252**	***mxm@cll.com***
Raphael Nemes	**(212) 790-9248**	***rxn@cll.com***
Reema Pangarkar	**(212) 790-9229**	***rxp@cll.com***
Joel K. Schmidt	**(212) 790-9244**	***jks@cll.com***
Maria A. Scungio	**(212) 790-9253**	***mys@cll.com***
Eric J. Shimanoff	**(212) 790-9226**	***ejs@cll.com***
Adam D. Siegartel	**(212) 790-9224**	***ads@cll.com***
Deborah K. Squiers	**(212) 790-9211**	***dks@cll.com***
Emily F. Stein	**(212) 790-9271**	***efs@cll.com***
John J. Torrente	**(212) 790-9273**	***jjt@cll.com***
Brian R. Volk	**(212) 790-9282**	***brv@cll.com***
Lyndsey Waddington	**(212) 790-9214**	***lxw@cll.com***
Dorothy R. Whitney	**(212) 790-9212**	***drw@cll.com***
Fei Xing	**(212) 790-9254**	***fxx@cll.com***
Anastasia Zhading	**(212) 790-9286**	***axz@cll.com***

www.ingramcontent.com/pod-product-compliance
Lightning Source LLC
Chambersburg PA
CBHW050528240926
51846CB00003B/744
9781967505012